CONTENT ESSENTIALS™ for Science

Vocabulary

Content

Literacy

Mc Graw Hill **Wright Group**

The *McGraw·Hill* Companies

www.WrightGroup.com

Send all inquiries to:
Wright Group/McGraw-Hill
P.O. Box 812960
Chicago, IL 60681

ISBN 978-1-4045-6738-2
MHID 1-4045-6738-0

1 2 3 4 5 6 7 8 9 QWD 13 12 11 10 09 08 07

The **McGraw·Hill** Companies

Author

Margarita Calderón, Ph.D.
Senior Research Scientist and Professor
Johns Hopkins University

Consultant Reviewer

James A. Shymansky, Ph.D.
E. Desmond Lee Professor of Science
   Education
University of Missouri St. Louis

Reviewers

Amy Diedrichsen Bates
Curriculum Specialist
Plano Independent School District
Plano, Texas

Lillian Vega Castaneda, Ed.D.
Professor, Language, Culture, and Literacy
California State University,
Channel Islands

Susan Greca
Director of Second Language Programs
Freeport Public Schools
Freeport, New York

Elizabeth Jiménez
English Learner Consultant
GEMAS Consulting Co.
Pomona, California

Sandra Ann Madriaga
Supervisor of World Languages,
   English As A Second Language
   and High Ability Programs
Evansville-Vanderburgh School Corporation
Evansville, Indiana

Janie Perez Martin
Physics Instructor
Southwest Independent School District
San Antonio, Texas

Vyagale D. Maryland
Title III/ESL & Languages Other Than
   English Specialist
Montgomery Public Schools
Curriculum and Instruction
Montgomery, Alabama

Ann L. Rifleman
Teacher
Mesa Unified School District
Arizona

Elma Alicia Ruiz
Humanities Coordinator
Denver Public Schools, Department of
   Teaching and Learning
Denver, Colorado

Linda Thompson, Ed.D.
Director of Curriculum, Instruction,
   and Assessment
Carmel Clay Schools
Carmel, Indiana

Contents

PHYSICAL SCIENCE **154**

STUDYING SCIENCE **202**

Part Two Literacy Essentials 226

READING SCIENCE 228

COMPREHENSION 246

How to Use This Book

Your book has two parts. You can use the first part to learn about science topics. If you need help reading or writing about science, use the second part.

Part One Science Essentials

LIFE SCIENCE Life science is the study of living things. You will learn about many types of living things, what they are made of, and how they live.

EARTH SCIENCE Earth science is the study of many topics. It includes what makes up Earth and facts about fossils, weather, water, and space.

PHYSICAL SCIENCE Physical science is the study of matter and energy. These lessons explain matter and how energy causes change.

STUDYING SCIENCE Science is about asking and answering questions. These lessons show you how scientists solve problems.

Part Two Literacy Essentials

READING SCIENCE The lessons in this section show you how to use text features to help you read.

COMPREHENSION These lessons teach you strategies and skills for reading.

UNDERSTANDING LANGUAGE This section helps you learn phrases and words in the English language.

WRITING FOR SCIENCE The lessons in this section show you how to write a science report.

HOW TO USE THIS BOOK

Previewing Lessons

Each lesson has the same text features, such as an Essential Idea, photographs, labels, and Why It Matters to help students easily find and comprehend the topic information.

Essential Idea
The Essential Idea tells you what the lesson is all about.

photographs
Photographs help you visualize the topic.

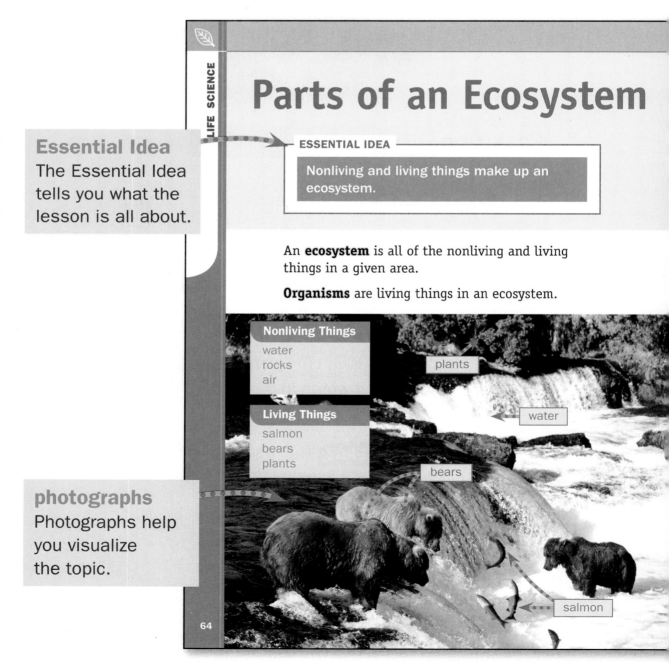

LIFE SCIENCE

Parts of an Ecosystem

ESSENTIAL IDEA

Nonliving and living things make up an ecosystem.

An **ecosystem** is all of the nonliving and living things in a given area.

Organisms are living things in an ecosystem.

Nonliving Things
water
rocks
air

Living Things
salmon
bears
plants

plants

water

bears

salmon

64

12

Learning Academic Vocabulary

You need to know academic vocabulary, or words used in school subjects, to learn. Each lesson highlights the words you will need to understand ideas in science.

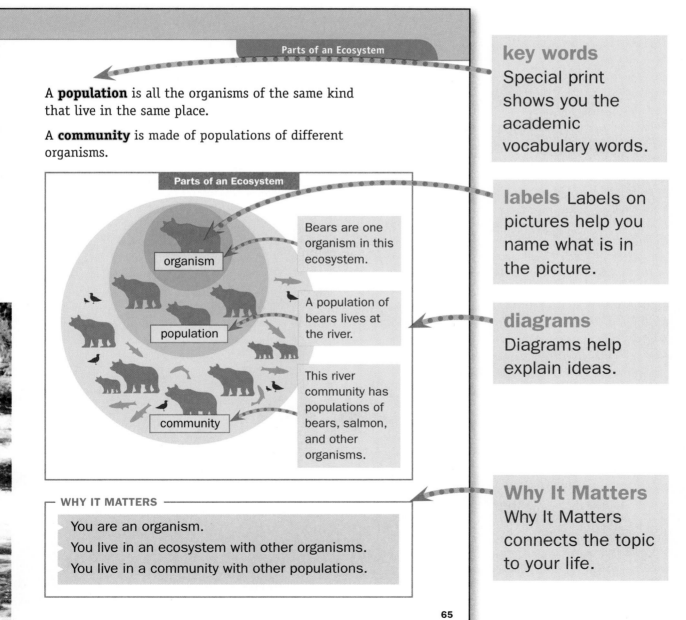

Parts of an Ecosystem

A **population** is all the organisms of the same kind that live in the same place.

A **community** is made of populations of different organisms.

Parts of an Ecosystem

organism

Bears are one organism in this ecosystem.

population

A population of bears lives at the river.

community

This river community has populations of bears, salmon, and other organisms.

WHY IT MATTERS

You are an organism.
You live in an ecosystem with other organisms.
You live in a community with other populations.

65

key words
Special print shows you the academic vocabulary words.

labels Labels on pictures help you name what is in the picture.

diagrams Diagrams help explain ideas.

Why It Matters Why It Matters connects the topic to your life.

Part One

Science Essentials

In this part of the book, you will learn all about the basics of science.

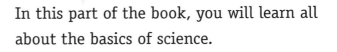
Life science is the study of living things. You will learn about many types of living things, what they are made of, and how they live.

Earth science is the study of many topics. It includes what makes up Earth and facts about fossils, weather, water, and space.

Physical science is the study of matter and energy. These lessons explain matter and how energy causes change.

Science is about asking and answering questions. These lessons show you how scientists solve problems.

Classifying Organisms

ESSENTIAL IDEA

Scientists classify living things into groups. The organisms in each group have traits in common.

All living things are **organisms**. Scientists put organisms into groups, called **kingdoms**.

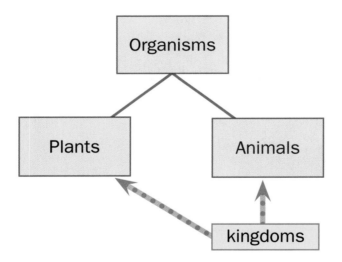

Scientists classify organisms based on the **traits**, or characteristics, they have in common.

kingdom	traits
plants	stay in one place
animals	move from place to place

Kingdoms and Species

Many kinds of organisms are in a kingdom. Kingdoms are divided into many smaller groups. **Species** is the smallest group in a kingdom. It includes only one kind of organism.

Bears and humans are both in the animal kingdom. They are in different species.

bear

human

WHY IT MATTERS

> You are an organism.
> You belong to the animal kingdom.
> You are a member of the human species.

Animal Groups

ESSENTIAL IDEA

There are two main groups of animals. One group of animals has backbones. The other group does not have backbones.

Scientists divide animals into two main groups: vertebrates and invertebrates.

Vertebrates

Animals with **backbones** are **vertebrates**. Fish, snakes, and frogs are animals with backbones.

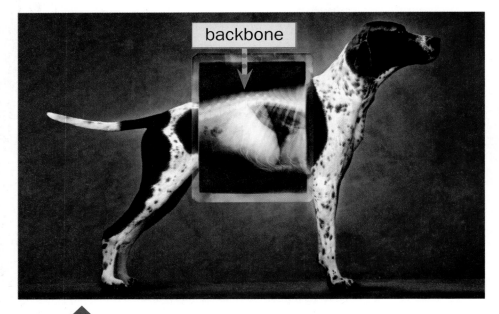

backbone

A dog has a backbone.

Invertebrates

Animals without backbones are **invertebrates**. Spiders, insects, and jellyfish are animals without backbones.

Arthropods make up the largest group of invertebrates.

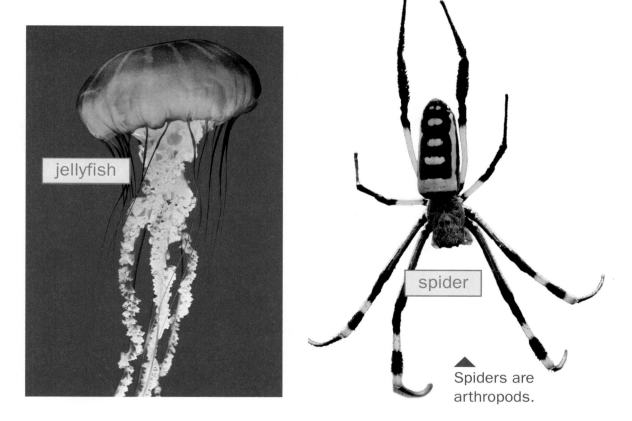

jellyfish

spider

▲ Spiders are arthropods.

WHY IT MATTERS

You are a vertebrate because you have a backbone. Most animals do not have backbones.

Types of Animals

There are five main types of animals with backbones.

Each type of animal shares the same traits.

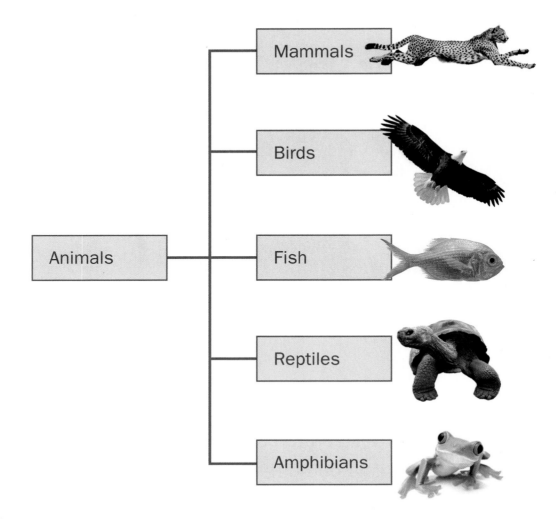

Mammals

Mammals are **warm-blooded** animals. Their bodies stay at about the same temperature all the time.

All mammals breathe with **lungs**. Hair or **fur** covers all mammals. They have **limbs**.

Mammal traits

Mammals are warm-blooded.
Mammals breathe with lungs.
Mammals have hair or fur.
Mammals have limbs.

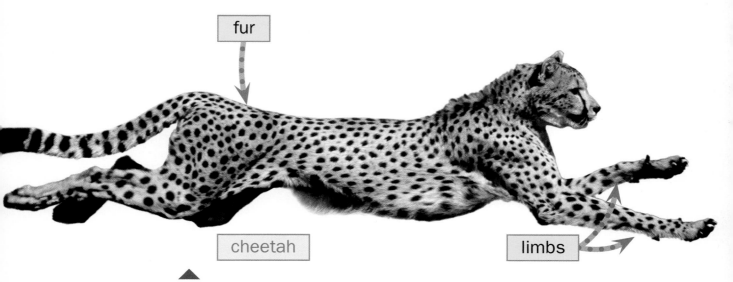

fur

cheetah

limbs

▲ A cheetah is a mammal. Its fur has spots. It uses limbs to run.

more about **Types of Animals**

LIFE SCIENCE

Birds

All **birds** have **feathers** and **wings**. Feathers cover a bird's body. Most birds use wings to fly through the air.

eagle

Other birds do not fly. Penguins use their wings to swim.

feathers

penguins

wings

Bird traits

Birds are warm-blooded.
Birds have feathers.
Birds have wings.
Some birds fly.

Fish

Fish live in the water their whole lives. They have **gills** to breathe under water. Most fish have **fins** to swim.

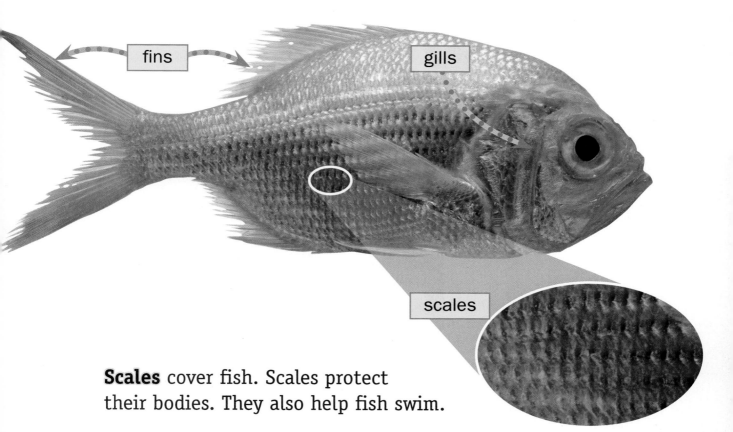

fins

gills

scales

Scales cover fish. Scales protect their bodies. They also help fish swim.

Fish traits

Most fish are cold-blooded.
Fish have gills to breathe under water.
Most fish have fins to help them swim.
Most fish have scales to protect their bodies.

LIFE SCIENCE

Reptiles

Reptiles are **cold-blooded** animals. Their body temperature is the same as the temperature around them.

snake

scales

tortoise

shell

Reptile traits

Reptiles are cold-blooded.
Reptiles breathe with lungs.
Reptiles have scales, rough skin, or shells.

Amphibians

Amphibians are born in water. They have gills to breathe in the water. As they grow, their bodies change from one form to another. Amphibians live on land as adults. They breathe with lungs.

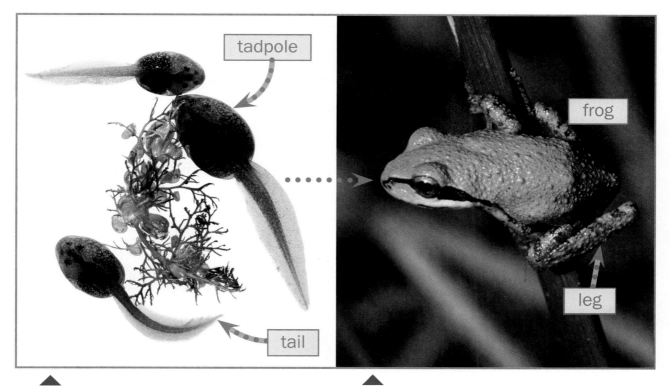

tadpole

tail

frog

leg

▲ Tadpoles have tails. Tadpoles grow into frogs.

▲ A frog is an adult. A frog has legs.

WHY IT MATTERS

You have hair on your head, arms, and legs.

You are warm-blooded.

You are a mammal.

Animal Needs

ESSENTIAL IDEA

Animals have basic needs. An animal gets what it needs from its environment.

All animals need **energy**, **water**, **shelter**, or a place to live, and **oxygen**. Animals get all of these things from their **environments**.

An environment includes everything around an animal, including living and nonliving things.

water Most animals drink water from lakes, rivers, and ponds.

energy Food gives animals the energy their bodies need.

shelter A shelter protects an animal from weather and other animals.

oxygen Mammals and birds get oxygen by breathing in air.

WHY IT MATTERS

▷ You need food, water, oxygen, and shelter.

▷ You get what you need from your environment.

29

Animal Life Cycles

ESSENTIAL IDEA

All animals reproduce. A life cycle includes all the stages of an animal's life.

All animals go through the **stages** of a life cycle. Adults **reproduce** to make offspring, or babies. A life cycle begins when the offspring are **born**.

The offspring **grow** and become **adults**. Then the adults produce new offspring, and the life cycle continues.

Animals are born in different ways.

Elephants and most other mammals grow inside their mothers' bodies before they are born.

adult

baby

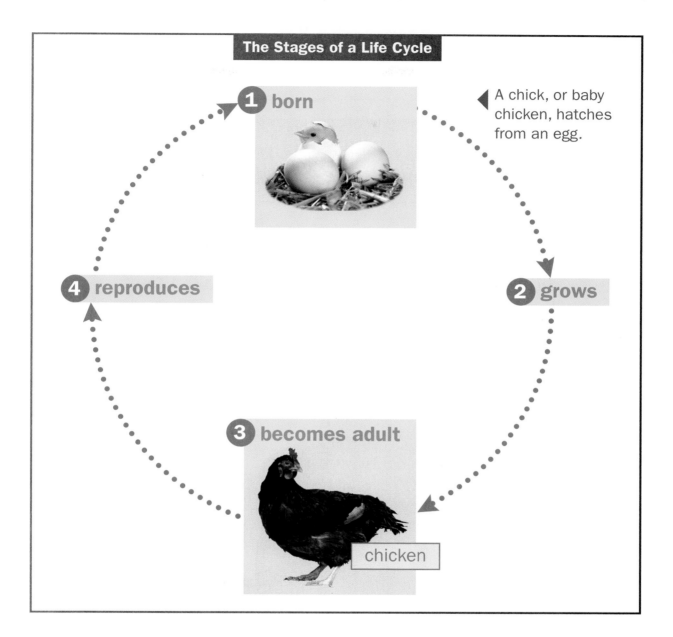

The Stages of a Life Cycle

1 born

A chick, or baby chicken, hatches from an egg.

2 grows

4 reproduces

3 becomes adult

chicken

WHY IT MATTERS

You are in a stage of your life cycle.

You are a mammal and grew in your mother's body before you were born.

Plant Needs

ESSENTIAL IDEA

All plants share the same needs. Unlike animals, plants can make their own food.

Plants need **water**, **nutrients**, **light**, and **carbon dioxide** from the air to live. Plants make their own food.

Plants turn light, air, and water into food.

Plant Needs

carbon dioxide Air provides plants with carbon dioxide. This gas comes out of your lungs when you breathe. Plants use carbon dioxide to make food.

light The Sun gives plants the light they need to live. Plants turn sunlight into food.

water and nutrients Water provides plants with nutrients. Nutrients help plants live and grow.

WHY IT MATTERS

Like plants, you need air, water, and food.

Plants use the carbon dioxide that you breathe out.

Parts of Plants

Plants have parts that help them to live.

Most plants have the same **parts**. They are a **stem**, **leaves**, and **roots**. Each part has an important **role**, or job. The parts work together to help the plant live and grow.

Plant Parts and Their Roles

part	roles
stem	holds up leaves and flowers
leaves	make food
roots	hold plant in soil take in water and nutrients

WHY IT MATTERS

Like plants, you have parts that have different roles, or jobs.

stem Plants have a stem that holds up the leaves and flowers.

leaves Plants use leaves to make food. Most leaves are green.

roots Roots hold the plant in the soil. They also absorb, or take in, water and nutrients from the soil.

35

Plant Groups

ESSENTIAL IDEA

Scientists group plants by the kinds of parts they have or by how they reproduce.

One way scientists group, or classify, plants is by their parts.

Plants without Tubes

Nonvascular plants do not have tubes. They grow in wet places. They do not grow very large or tall.

moss

Nonvascular plants
don't have tubes
can't grow tall

▲ Moss is a nonvascular plant. It does not have tubes for moving water.

Plants with Tubes

Most plants have **tubes** in their roots, stems, and leaves. The tubes in the roots **absorb**, or take in, water and carry it to the stems and leaves.

Plants with tubes are called **vascular** plants.

tubes

▲ Vascular plants can grow very tall because tubes carry water through the plants.

absorb

Vascular plants

have tubes in roots, stems, and leaves

can grow tall

more about **Plant Groups** **37**

LIFE SCIENCE

Scientists group vascular plants by how they reproduce.

Seed Plants

Some vascular plants make seeds inside **flowers**. Others make seeds inside **cones**.

Plants that grow seeds inside flowers are called **flowering plants**. Plants that grow seeds inside cones are called **conifers**.

flowering plant

flowers

conifer

cones

Nonseed Plants

Some vascular plants, like ferns, make **spores** instead of flowers and cones.

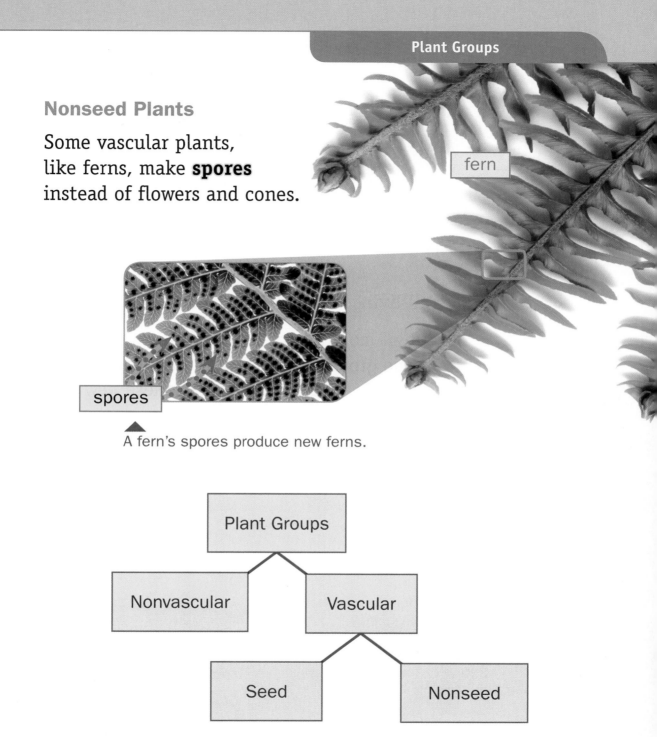

fern

spores

▲ A fern's spores produce new ferns.

Plant Groups

Nonvascular

Vascular

Seed

Nonseed

WHY IT MATTERS

You can classify plants by the parts they have and by how they reproduce.

Plant Life Cycles

ESSENTIAL IDEA

Plants go through a life cycle.

Like all living things, plants have a life **cycle**.

The life of most plants begins with a seed. Some seeds fall to the ground. The wind and animals help to **scatter** seeds. **Seedlings** grow in these new places.

1 **seed** The seed germinates, or starts to grow. The seed breaks open. A seedling sprouts, or comes up.

2 **seedling** The seedling grows. Roots grow from the bottom. A stem sprouts from the top.

seed

seedling

stem

Seeds need soil, water, and the right temperature to start growing, or **germinate**.

WHY IT MATTERS

You go through a life cycle.

3 **stem and leaves**
The stem pushes above the soil. It grows leaves. The roots grow longer and deeper.

4 **new seed** The young plant grows into an adult plant that can reproduce.

stem

leaves

root

roots

41

What Flowers Do

Flowers help plants reproduce.

Many plants form seeds inside flowers. A flower has parts that help a plant **reproduce**.

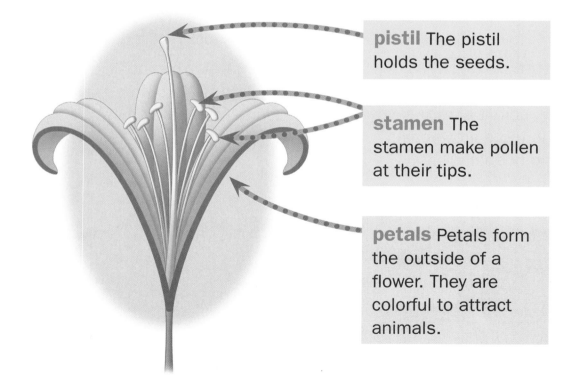

pistil The pistil holds the seeds.

stamen The stamen make pollen at their tips.

petals Petals form the outside of a flower. They are colorful to attract animals.

Animals, like bees, can help **pollinate** the flower. The **pollen** sticks to their bodies as they look for food.

As animals travel from flower to flower, they carry the pollen from the **stamen** of one flower to the **pistil** of another.

After a flower is pollinated, the seed forms in the pistil.

bee

petal

▲
The bright colors of flower petals attract animals, like bees.

Steps of pollination

1. Stamen make pollen.
2. Pollen sticks to an animal.
3. Animals can carry pollen to a pistil on another flower.
4. Seeds grow in pistil.

WHY IT MATTERS

You eat the seeds that some flowers make.

How Plants Make Food

Plants make their own food through a process called photosynthesis.

A plant can make its own food. It uses a **process** called **photosynthesis**. A process is a way of doing something.

Chlorophyll is in a plant's leaves. Chlorophyll uses the Sun's energy to **combine**, or put together, **carbon dioxide** and **water**. This forms a sugar for the plant's food.

The plant's leaves give off oxygen into the air you breathe.

Leaves take in energy from the Sun and carbon dioxide from the air.

The plant's leaves make sugar.

Roots take in water. Tubes in the stem carry the water to the leaves.

WHY IT MATTERS

You can't make food in your body, but plants can. You breathe in the oxygen that plants give off.

Adaptations in Living Things

ESSENTIAL IDEA

Living things are adapted to their environment to help them survive.

An **adaptation** is a trait that helps a living thing **survive** in its environment. Animals and plants **inherit**, or get, these traits from their parents.

Adaptations

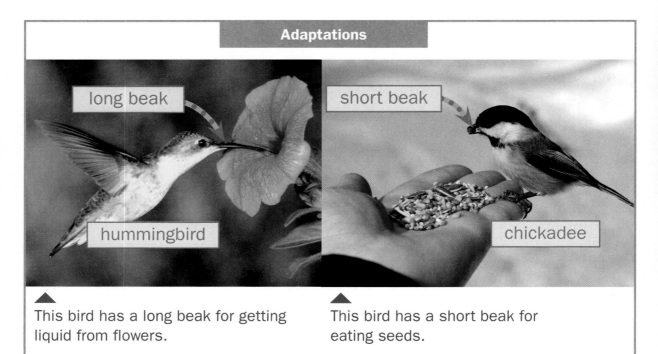

long beak

hummingbird

short beak

chickadee

▲ This bird has a long beak for getting liquid from flowers.

▲ This bird has a short beak for eating seeds.

The color and shape of an animal can be adaptations that help it survive. The way an animal **behaves**, or acts, can also help it survive.

insect

◀ This insect looks like a twig. Birds and larger insects can't see it.

Antelopes live together to protect one another. ▼

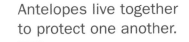

antelopes

more about **Adaptations in Living Things**

Plants

Plants have **adapted** to many different **environments**. They may get little sunlight or lots of it. It may rain a lot or very little.

ivy

▲ Plants under big trees get little sunlight. Ivy climbs up trees to reach the sunlight.

Plants in hot, dry environments have adapted to get water.

cactus

▲
The roots of cactus plants spread out to reach water.
Their long, thick stems hold water.

WHY IT MATTERS

> You have traits that help you survive in your environment.

Cells and What They Do

Cells are important to life. The jobs cells do help keep an organism alive.

All living things are made up of **cells**. Each cell has a **membrane**, a **nucleus**, **cytoplasm**, and **organelles**.

muscle cells

Cells are very small. A microscope helps us see cells.

microscope

The parts of a cell do different jobs.

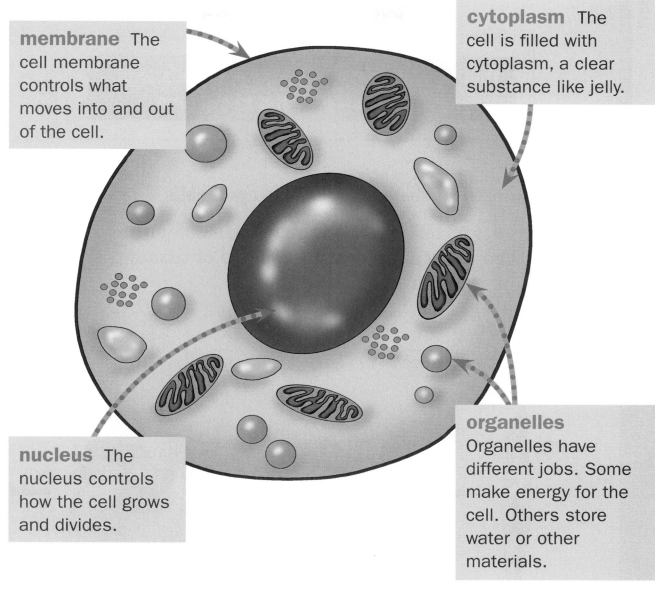

membrane The cell membrane controls what moves into and out of the cell.

cytoplasm The cell is filled with cytoplasm, a clear substance like jelly.

nucleus The nucleus controls how the cell grows and divides.

organelles Organelles have different jobs. Some make energy for the cell. Others store water or other materials.

WHY IT MATTERS

Your body contains cells that do different jobs.
Your muscle cells help you move.

Human Body Systems

ESSENTIAL IDEA

Your body is made up of cells, tissues, and organs. They work together in systems.

All parts of the body are made up of **cells**.

Groups of cells that do the same kind of job are called **tissues**. An **organ** is a group of tissues that work together to do a job.

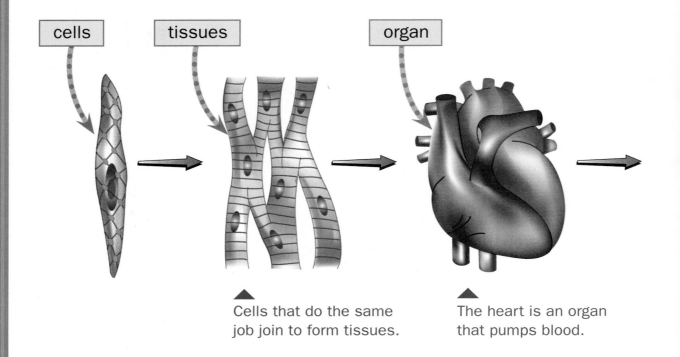

cells   tissues   organ

Cells that do the same job join to form tissues.

The heart is an organ that pumps blood.

Organs work together in a **system**. Your heart works with other organs in a system to move blood around your body.

Your **body** contains a number of organ systems. Each system does a job like helping you move, eat, or breathe.

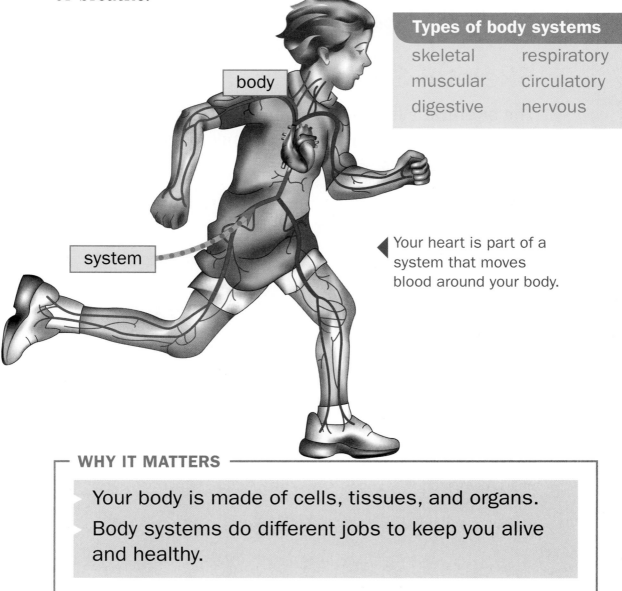

body

system

Types of body systems

skeletal	respiratory
muscular	circulatory
digestive	nervous

◄ Your heart is part of a system that moves blood around your body.

─ WHY IT MATTERS ─

> Your body is made of cells, tissues, and organs.

> Body systems do different jobs to keep you alive and healthy.

How Your Body Moves

ESSENTIAL IDEA

The skeletal system and the muscular system help your body move.

Skeletal System

The **skeletal system** gives your body shape. Your **skeleton** is a system of **bones**. Some bones protect your body organs.

The place where bones come together is called a **joint**.

skeleton

bones

muscles

Some joints can only move up and down. Other joints can twist and turn.

joint

Muscular System

The **muscular system** helps your body move. Bones can't move by themselves. **Muscles** are tissues attached to the bones. Muscle cells can change their length to help move bones.

arm

leg

Muscles work in pairs. As one muscle gets longer, the other one gets shorter. This is how you can bend and straighten your arm or leg.

WHY IT MATTERS

Bones and muscles in your body let you move.

Your bones and muscles work together.

How You Get Nutrients

ESSENTIAL IDEA

The digestive system sends nutrients to all systems in your body.

Digestive System

Food contains nutrients that give the body energy to move, grow, and live.

Organs in the **digestive system** include the **mouth**, the **esophagus**, the **stomach**, and the **intestines**.

Where Food Moves

1 mouth

2 esophagus

3 stomach

4 intestines

The digestive system **digests**, or breaks down, food.
Then it sends nutrients to all parts of the body.

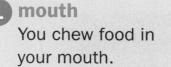

1 mouth
You chew food in
your mouth.

2 esophagus
When you
swallow, food
moves down your
esophagus to
your stomach.

3 stomach
Stomach muscles
mix the food with
juices and
change it into
a thick paste.

4 intestines
Nutrients pass
through the walls
of the intestines
into the blood.
Blood carries the
nutrients to the
cells in the body.

WHY IT MATTERS

> You eat food to give your body nutrients.
>
> Nutrients give you energy to play games or
> study in school.

How Oxygen and Nutrients Move

ESSENTIAL IDEA

The respiratory and circulatory systems deliver oxygen and nutrients to the cells in your body.

Respiratory System

Cells need oxygen and nutrients to do their work. You get oxygen when you **breathe**.

Organs in your **respiratory system** include the **nose**, **windpipe**, **lungs**, and **capillaries**.

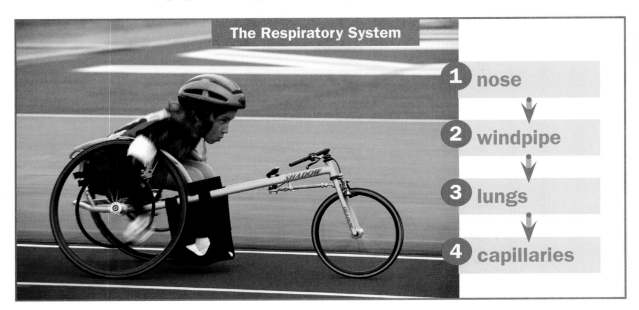

The Respiratory System

1 nose

2 windpipe

3 lungs

4 capillaries

The respiratory system moves oxygen into your blood.

1 **nose** Your nose traps dust and warms the air you breathe in.

2 **windpipe** Air travels down your windpipe.

3 **lungs** As air enters the lungs, it goes into millions of tiny air sacs.

4 **capillaries** The air sacs are surrounded by capillaries—tiny blood vessels. Oxygen moves from the air sacs into the blood.

more about **How Oxygen and Nutrients Move**

Circulatory System

Your **circulatory system** is made up of your **heart**, **veins**, and **arteries**.

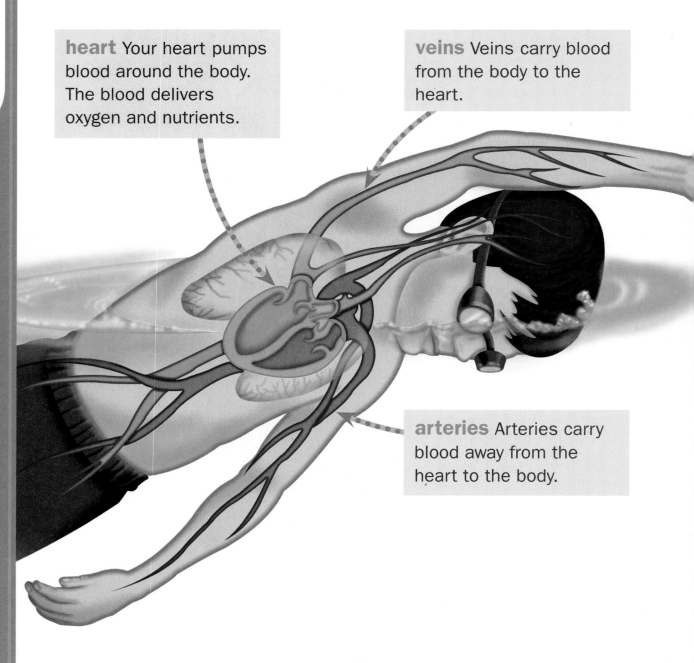

heart Your heart pumps blood around the body. The blood delivers oxygen and nutrients.

veins Veins carry blood from the body to the heart.

arteries Arteries carry blood away from the heart to the body.

The heart is a strong muscle. It pumps blood through your body. Veins carry blood to the heart. Arteries carry blood away from the heart.

heart

Body Systems and Their Parts

Respiratory system	Circulatory system
nose	heart
windpipe	blood
lungs	veins
capillaries	arteries

WHY IT MATTERS

> Your body's cells need oxygen to do their work.
>
> Breathing brings air into your body.
>
> Your lungs take oxygen from the air and send it to your blood.

How You Move and React

ESSENTIAL IDEA

The nervous system sends and receives messages. The messages help all parts of the body work together.

Nervous System

The **nervous system** controls how you move, think, and **react**. It senses changes in and around your body.

The Nervous System

The main parts of your nervous system are your **brain**, **spinal cord**, and **nerves**.

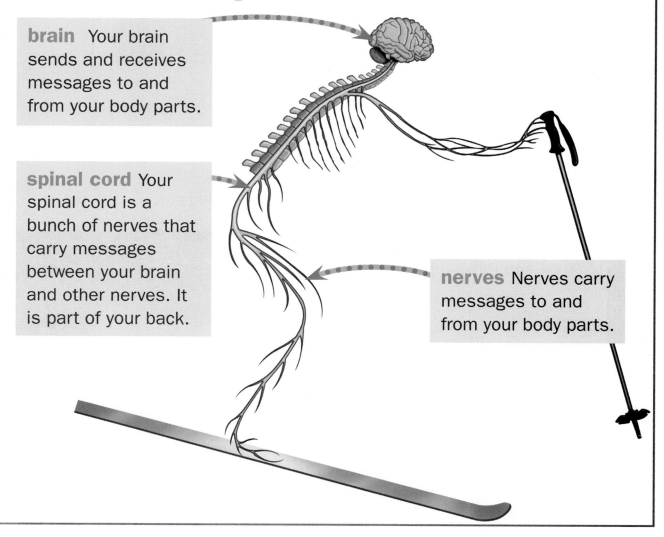

brain Your brain sends and receives messages to and from your body parts.

spinal cord Your spinal cord is a bunch of nerves that carry messages between your brain and other nerves. It is part of your back.

nerves Nerves carry messages to and from your body parts.

WHY IT MATTERS

Your brain controls how you move.

Your nervous system lets you move and react.

Parts of an Ecosystem

ESSENTIAL IDEA

Nonliving and living things make up an ecosystem.

An **ecosystem** is all of the nonliving and living things in a given area.

Organisms are living things in an ecosystem.

Nonliving Things
water
rocks
air

Living Things
salmon
bears
plants

plants

water

bears

salmon

A **population** is all the organisms of the same kind that live in the same place.

A **community** is made of populations of different organisms.

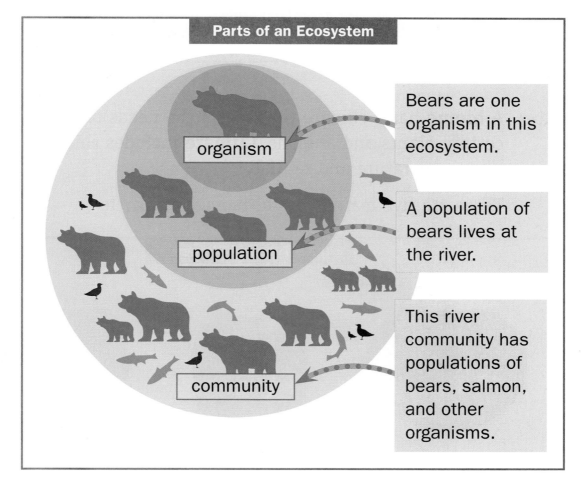

Parts of an Ecosystem

organism

Bears are one organism in this ecosystem.

population

A population of bears lives at the river.

community

This river community has populations of bears, salmon, and other organisms.

WHY IT MATTERS

> You are an organism.
> You live in an ecosystem with other organisms.
> You live in a community with other populations.

Kinds of Biomes

Organisms can only survive in biomes that meet their needs.

A **biome** has a climate that meets the needs of certain plants and animals. **Climate** includes things like temperature and rainfall.

There are five main types of biomes on Earth.

Five Types of Biomes

tropical rain forest

desert

forest

tundra

grassland

Tropical Rain Forest

The **tropical rain forest** biome gets a lot of rainfall and has high temperatures. Tropical rain forests contain more different kinds of organisms than any other biome.

flowers

frog

bird

Colorful birds, flowers, and frogs live in a rain forest.

Desert

Deserts are very **dry** and get little rain. Few plants grow there, so there is little shade. Some deserts get very hot during the day.

Sand and rocks cover deserts.

Cacti, shrubs, and coyotes can live in deserts.

▼

desert

coyote

shrubs

Grassland

Grasslands are usually warm. They are not as dry as deserts, but they are drier than forests.

Grasslands are covered by grasses and wildflowers.

bison

grassland

▲
Bison graze in grasslands.

LIFE SCIENCE

Forest

Forests have many trees. In some forests, trees lose their leaves in the winter. Forests get plenty of water or snow.

forest

trees

▲ Some trees in forests lose their leaves in the winter.

Tundra

The **tundra** is the coldest biome on Earth. Snow and ice cover a tundra for most of the year. Very few plants can grow in this cold, dry place.

tundra

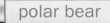
polar bear

Polar bears have thick fur to keep them warm in a tundra.

WHY IT MATTERS

You live in a biome that meets your needs.

71

Types of Living Things

ESSENTIAL IDEA

Organisms get their energy in two different ways. Producers make their own food. Consumers eat other organisms.

All living things need energy from food to survive.

Producers

Producers, like plants, make their own food. Energy from the Sun is turned into food.

zebra

producers

grass

▲ Grass is a producer. It makes its own food from the Sun. Zebras are not producers.

Consumers

Animals like zebras can't make their own food. They are **consumers** which must eat other living things to get their energy.

Living things in a community **interact** to get food. A consumer that eats other animals is called a **predator**.

The **prey** is the animal the predator kills and eats.

The lion is a predator. It gets its energy from eating zebras, one of its prey.

predator

prey

lion

zebra

LIFE SCIENCE

Types of Consumers

Consumers are divided into groups by the type of food they eat.

Herbivores

Herbivores get all their energy by eating plants. For example, zebras and elephants eat grasses. Elephants eat leaves and grass.

herbivore

elephant

Carnivores

Carnivores get all their energy by eating other animals. Frogs are carnivores that eat insects.

carnivore

frog

insect

Omnivores

Omnivores get energy by eating both plants and animals. Gorillas, chimps, and some monkeys eat both plants and insects.

omnivore

chimp

Scavengers

Scavengers feed on dead animals that they did not kill. Vultures and hyenas eat animals that other carnivores killed and left behind. Scavengers also feed on animals that die naturally.

scavenger

hyena

LIFE SCIENCE

Decomposers

Living things called **decomposers** feed on dead plants and animals.

Decomposers include **bacteria**, insects in the soil, and **fungi**. Some types of fungi are mold and mushrooms.

These organisms **recycle**, or break down, things into simple chemicals. Producers, like plants, can reuse these nutrients from the soil.

decomposers

mushrooms

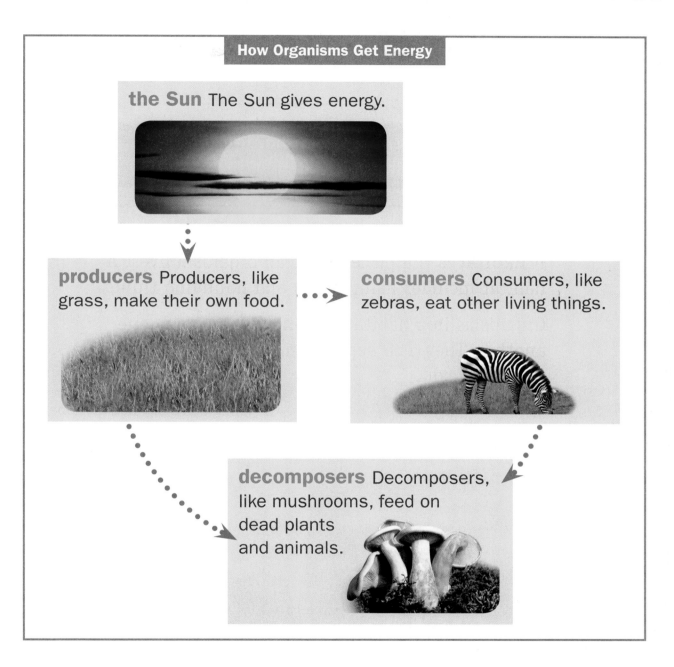

How Organisms Get Energy

the Sun The Sun gives energy.

producers Producers, like grass, make their own food.

consumers Consumers, like zebras, eat other living things.

decomposers Decomposers, like mushrooms, feed on dead plants and animals.

WHY IT MATTERS

You eat plants and animals to get energy.

You are a consumer.

Habitats

ESSENTIAL IDEA

Living things make their home in a place called a habitat.

A **habitat** is the place where an organism lives. A habitat includes many living and nonliving things.

Organisms in a habitat **depend** on, or need, one another. They also depend on nonliving things, like water and soil.

Humans in a city habitat depend on other people to provide food, clothing, and other services.

habitat

city

Each organism does different jobs in a habitat.
A **niche** is the role an organism has in its habitat.

Organisms in a habitat have a **relationship**.

swamp

plants

egret

▲ In a swamp habitat, plants provide food.
They give fish and insects a place to hide.
An egret eats fish and insects in a swamp.

— WHY IT MATTERS —

> You live in a habitat.

> You depend on other living and nonliving things in your habitat.

How Living Things Interact

ESSENTIAL IDEA

Living things in a habitat either help one another or compete with one another.

All living things have needs. As organisms **interact**, they sometimes help one another meet their needs.

▲ Rabbits feed on grass. The grass hides the rabbits from predators.

▲
Deer feed on grass and nuts. Deer compete for food.

Individuals in a habitat sometimes **compete** with one another for **resources**, like food.

If there aren't enough resources for an individual to survive, it will die or move to another area.

Symbiosis is a close **relationship** between two different species. The species interact with one another over a long time.

Symbiosis can help two organisms.

butterfly

flower

The flower gives the butterfly food. The butterfly carries the flower's pollen.

Some organisms, called **parasites**, are harmful.
They hurt the **host**, or other organisms they live in.

▲ Mistletoe is a parasite that grows on trees and shrubs.

WHY IT MATTERS

Some organisms, like plants, help you meet your needs.

Some organisms, like biting insects, harm you.

83

Food Chains and Webs

ESSENTIAL IDEA

Energy moves through a habitat in a food chain.

The Sun is a natural source of energy. Energy moves from the producers to each consumer. This is called the food chain.

A **food chain** shows what organisms eat in a **habitat**. The arrows show how the energy moves to each organsim.

Sun

plant

mouse

snake

▲ The plant stores the energy from the Sun as food.

▲ The mouse eats the plant.

▲ The snake eats the mouse.

There are many food chains in a habitat. The food chains combine to form a **food web**. This food web shows the food chains in a forest habitat.

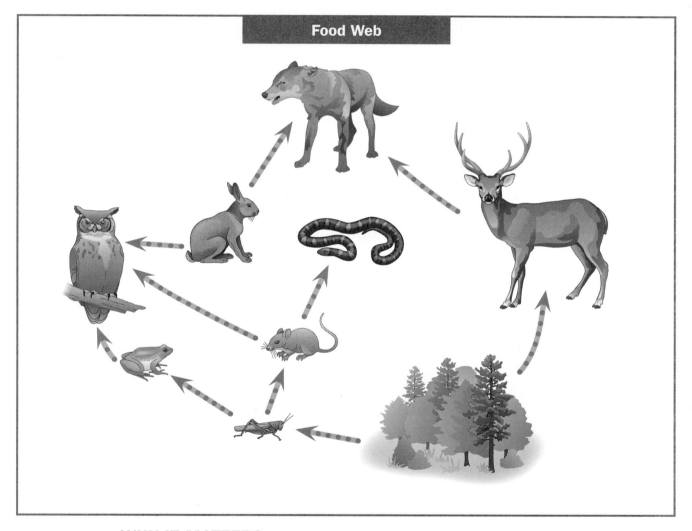

Food Web

WHY IT MATTERS

You are the top consumer in a food chain.

You can get more energy by eating producers than by eating other consumers.

Changes to Habitats

ESSENTIAL IDEA

When a habitat changes, some species can become endangered or extinct.

Animals may not be able to live in a habitat if it changes too much.

Natural events, like a volcano eruption, can **threaten** a habitat. People can threaten habitats too. For example, an oil spill will pollute an ocean habitat. This may make the animals sick and **endanger** a **species**.

bird

▲ Oil spills endanger sea birds, seals, and fish.

whale

▲
Some whale species are endangered
because their habitat is changing.

If people don't help an endangered species, the
population may become **extinct**. This means that
the species can no longer be found in nature.

WHY IT MATTERS

Some of your activities may threaten habitats.

People and the Environment

ESSENTIAL IDEA

Human activities affect environments.

Human activities **affect** the **environment** in many ways. For example, growing crops can bring more animals to an environment. Building homes and roads can destroy an environment.

crops

homes

road

Human activities cause many types of **pollution**. Cars give off **hazardous** gases. Factories produce smoke. Making things we use, like plastic, sometimes creates **waste chemicals**.

pollution

waste chemicals

▲
Waste chemicals enter streams and lakes. This harms fish and other species that live in the water.

WHY IT MATTERS

> Making and using some products causes pollution.
> You can reduce pollution by using products that don't hurt the environment.

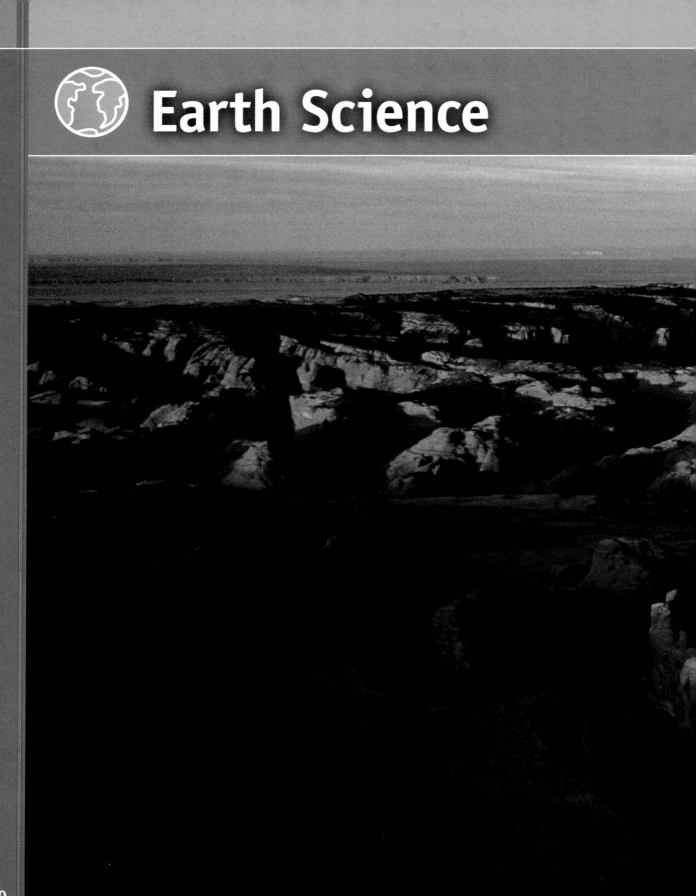

Earth Science

Earth's Layers

ESSENTIAL IDEA

Earth is made up of layers.

Earth is not the same all the way through. It is made of **layers.** The **crust** is the outside layer that covers Earth. The **mantle** is the middle layer. The **outer core** and **inner core** make up Earth's center.

The crust is the land you walk on. The land under the oceans is part of the crust, too.
▼

ocean

land

crust The crust is made of rocks and soil.

mantle The mantle is made of solid and melted rock.

outer core The outer core is liquid metal.

inner core The inner core is solid metal.

What Makes Up Earth	
layer	**made of**
crust	rocks and soil
mantle	solid and melted rock
outer core	liquid metal
inner core	solid metal

WHY IT MATTERS

You live on Earth's crust.

93

Rocks and Minerals

ESSENTIAL IDEA

Earth's crust is made up of rocks. Rocks contain minerals.

Rock makes up most of Earth's crust. When you look at a rock, you may see tiny **grains** of different colors. These grains are **minerals** that make up rocks.

minerals

◀ You can see different minerals in different rocks.

rocks

Minerals are nonliving, solid materials that form in the earth. Some minerals are soft, and some are hard.

Mineral Hardness

Talc is a very soft mineral.

talc

A diamond is a very hard mineral.

diamond

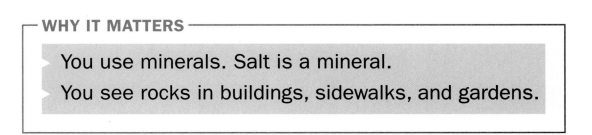

WHY IT MATTERS

You use minerals. Salt is a mineral.

You see rocks in buildings, sidewalks, and gardens.

Types of Rocks

ESSENTIAL IDEA

Scientists classify Earth's rocks by how they form.

Rocks form in three different ways.

Igneous Rocks

Igneous rock forms when melted rock hardens. Rocks deep below Earth's crust melt into **magma**.

When magma rises to Earth's surface, it is called **lava**. The lava cools and hardens into igneous rock.

Magma becomes lava when it rises out of deep cracks in Earth's crust.

lava

Metamorphic Rocks

Metamorphic rock forms when heat and **pressure** inside Earth change an existing rock.

How Metamorphic Rock Forms

The pressure may come from the weight of rocks pushing down on lower rock layers.

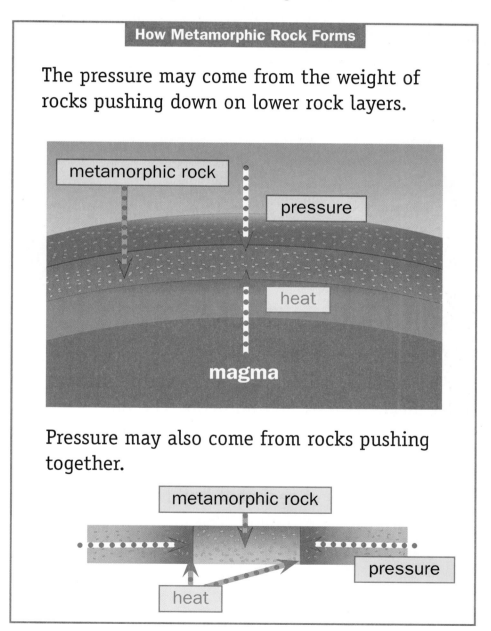

Pressure may also come from rocks pushing together.

sedimentary rock

Sedimentary Rocks

Wind and water **erode**, or wear away, rocks on Earth's surface. Rain carries away **sediment**, or loose pieces of rock and minerals. The pieces of sediment settle in layers, usually at the bottom of a river, lake, or ocean.

Over time, layers of sediment build up. Upper layers push down on lower layers. The lower layers change to **sedimentary rock**.

◀ Layers of sedimentary rock form over time. The layers of rock at the bottom are the oldest.

How Rocks Form

Each type of rock forms in a different way.

type of rocks	how they form
igneous	from lava that hardens
metamorphic	from heat and pressure
sedimentary	from sediment that settles in layers

WHY IT MATTERS

You can sometimes tell how a rock formed by looking at it.

Fossils

ESSENTIAL IDEA

Fossils are evidence of life that existed long ago.

Fossils form from **remains** of organisms that lived and died long ago. They show **evidence** of plants and animals that lived in the past.

All fossils form in sedimentary rock. Some fossils are skeletons of animals.

Fossils are proof that dinosaurs lived on Earth.

fossil

Other Types of Fossils

Some fossils are tracks, or footprints, animals left in mud that hardened into rock. Others are prints.

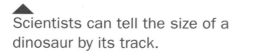

▲
Scientists can tell the size of a dinosaur by its track.

Plants may leave ▶ prints in rock.

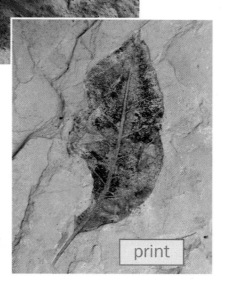

print

WHY IT MATTERS

Fossils let you see things that lived long ago.

You can learn about the history of Earth from fossils.

Landforms

ESSENTIAL IDEA

Earth's surface has many landforms.

A **landform** is a physical feature on Earth's surface. You can recognize a landform by its shape.

peak ➡

Mountains and Valleys

A **mountain** is a large mass of rock that sticks up from Earth's surface. Some mountains have sharp peaks, or tops. Others have rounded tops.

A **valley** is a low area of land between hills or mountains. A river often runs through a valley.

mountain

The Rocky Mountains in Montana have sharp, separate peaks.

valley

river

Canyons

A **canyon** is a deep, narrow valley with steep sides. Rivers often form canyons.

canyon

river

Plains

A **plain** is a wide area of flat or rolling land. It is usually lower than landforms around it. Plains cover much of the United States.

plain

WHY IT MATTERS

You can identify landforms by their shapes.

Changes to Earth's Surface

ESSENTIAL IDEA

Landforms are always changing. Some changes are gradual. Others are rapid.

Weathering

The Sun, rain, and wind cause **gradual**, or slow, changes in landforms. These changes are called **weathering**.

Heat from the Sun makes rocks **expand**, or get a little bigger. At night, the rocks cool off. They get a little smaller. Water in rocks sometimes freezes. These changes can make the rocks crack. Then pieces break off.

mountain

weathering

Erosion

Wind and water **erode** rock and may carry loose pieces and sediment away. This is called **erosion**.

The wind or water move sediment and deposit, or set it down somewhere. This is called **deposition**. Erosion and deposition gradually change the shape of the landform over many years.

landform

river

▲ The moving water in this river changes the shape of the landforms near it.

Glaciers

A **glacier** is a slow-moving river of ice and snow. Glaciers form in areas that stay cold all year. Snow builds up until it is very deep. Then it flows slowly downhill.

Rocks in the ice scrape the land below as the glacier moves. The glacier deposits, or leaves behind, sediment at its sides and bottom.

glacier

Landslides

Sometimes landforms change very fast. Weathering and erosion weaken rocks or soil on the side of a hill. Large amounts of rock and sediment may slide or fall all at once. This is called a **landslide**.

Heavy rain can change soil to mud. Soft mud begins to flow downhill. A mudslide can cause a **natural disaster**.

landslide

▲
This landslide buried many homes.

WHY IT MATTERS

> Weathering, glaciers, and landslides can change the land around you.

Volcanoes

Volcanoes form where there are very large cracks in Earth's crust. Pressure builds up in the magma and gases inside Earth. The magma and gases rise to the surface, and the volcano **erupts**.

lava

volcano

◀ As the lava cools, it becomes igneous rock.

Lava, the molten or liquid rock on the surface, flows over the land. Bits of **ash** and lava form a cone-shaped landform. The lava cools, and becomes hard rock.

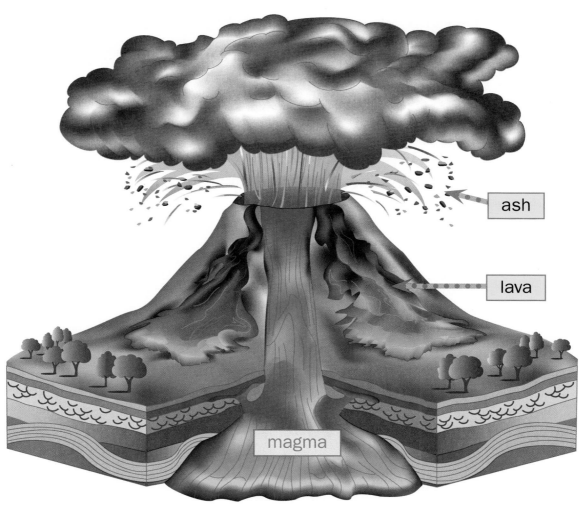

ash

lava

magma

WHY IT MATTERS

If you live near a volcano, the land around you might change quickly.

Earth's Plates

ESSENTIAL IDEA

> Earth's crust and upper mantle are made of plates that move.

Earth's crust and solid upper mantle are made up of huge **plates**. The plates are like pieces of a giant puzzle. The plates are moving very slowly all the time.

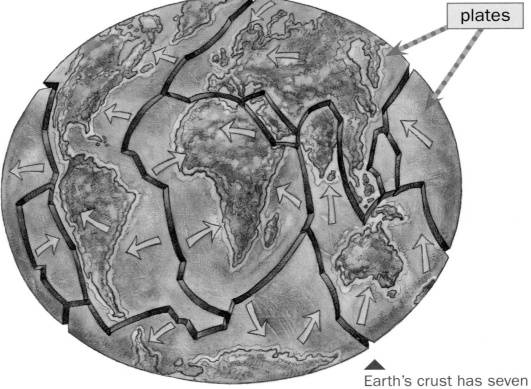

plates

▲ Earth's crust has seven large plates. It also has many smaller plates.

How Plates Move

Landforms, like mountains, form from movements of the plates. Some plates move toward one another. Some move away from one another. A **fault** is a place where two plates move past each other.

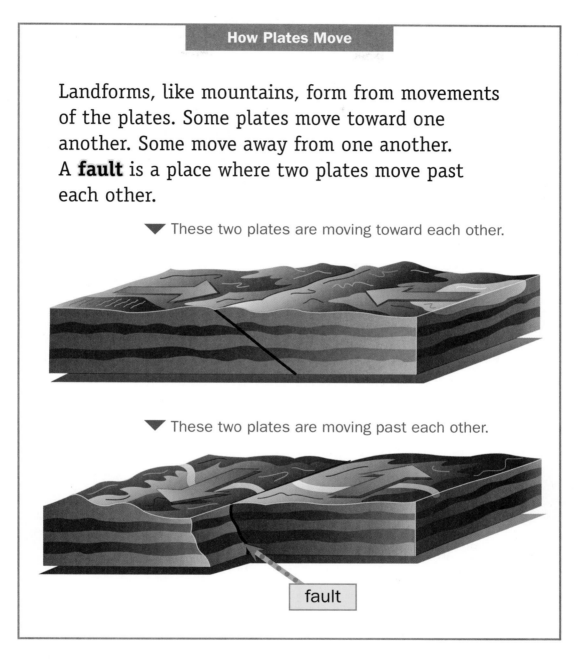

▼ These two plates are moving toward each other.

▼ These two plates are moving past each other.

fault

WHY IT MATTERS

You might not feel it, but Earth's plates are always moving.

Earthquakes

ESSENTIAL IDEA

When Earth's plates move past each other, pressure builds. The pressure is released as vibrations.

An **earthquake** is caused by sudden movements in Earth's crust. Pressure builds until the rocks break free and move. The sudden break causes **vibrations**. The vibrations travel through the whole Earth.

Earthquakes release a lot of energy. The energy can break apart buildings.

How Earthquakes Form

The place where the rock first breaks apart, or shifts, is called the **focus** of the earthquake. A point on Earth's surface above the focus is called the **epicenter**.

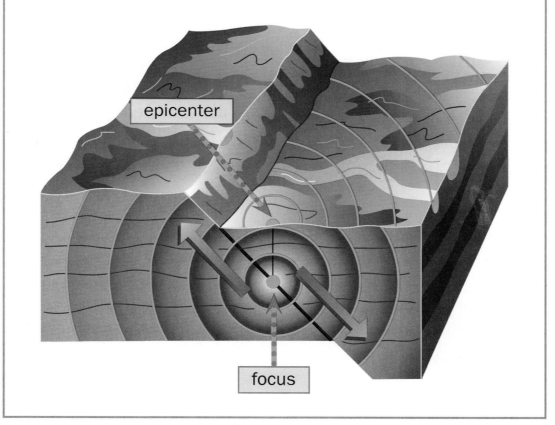

epicenter

focus

WHY IT MATTERS

You might have felt an earthquake where you live.

You should know what to do if an earthquake happens in your area.

Soil

Soil is made of loose, weathered rock and bits of decaying plant and animal material.

Soil forms when rock breaks into smaller pieces. Plants can grow in loose soil or in the cracks of rocks. When plants die and **decay**, they form **humus**.

Humus mixes with small bits of weathered rock called clay and sand. These materials form **loam**.

Soil that is rich in loam and humus is full of nutrients for farming.

▼

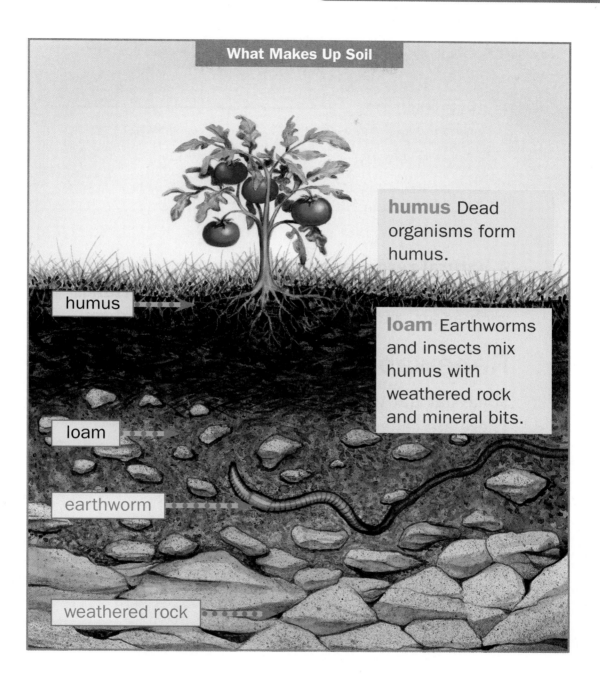

What Makes Up Soil

humus Dead organisms form humus.

humus

loam Earthworms and insects mix humus with weathered rock and mineral bits.

loam

earthworm

weathered rock

WHY IT MATTERS

The vegetables you eat are grown mostly in soil.

Earth's Resources

ESSENTIAL IDEA

Natural resources are found in the environment. They are essential for life.

A **natural resource** is any useful thing that is found in nature. Natural resources include things such as air, wind, water, trees, sunlight, and soil.

Renewable Resources

Some natural resources are used and then replaced. These are called **renewable resources**.

Trees are a renewable resource.

cut trees

plant trees

Many renewable resources provide **energy**. Humans use energy to make heat and light, and to run machines with electricity.

Water Dams use the energy from moving water to make electricity.

Sunlight These panels collect energy from the Sun. The energy can be changed to electricity.

Wind Wind turns the blades of these windmills. The movement is changed to electricity.

Nonrenewable Resources

Many of Earth's resources cannot be replaced.
There is a **limited** supply. After these resources are
used up there will be no more of them. These are
called **nonrenewable resources**.

mining

▲ Mining is a way to get minerals out of Earth's crust.
Minerals are a nonrenewable resource.

drilling

Humans drill for oil under Earth's crust. Earth contains several fossil fuels that humans use.

Gas, coal, and oil are nonrenewable resources called **fossil fuels**. They were made from plants and animals that died millions of years ago.

Burning fossil fuels, like oil, also called **petroleum**, releases their energy. Humans use a lot of energy. Humans are using up fossil fuels quickly.

WHY IT MATTERS

> You use natural resources like water to drink and wood or stones to make buildings.
>
> Some resources you use are limited.

121

Conservation and Recycling

ESSENTIAL IDEA

Conserving energy and recycling products can make Earth's resources last longer.

All the **products** humans use are made from natural resources. Paper is made from trees. Pots and pans are made from minerals.

Trash you throw away goes into **landfills**.

Landfills fill with trash fast when resources are not conserved.

landfill

You can **conserve**, or save, resources by using only as much as you need.

How to Recycle

Another way to conserve resources is to **recycle**. You can recycle products made of paper, plastic, aluminum, and glass.

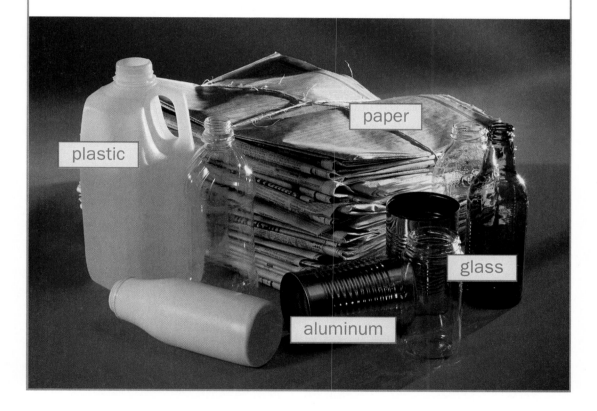

plastic

paper

glass

aluminum

WHY IT MATTERS

You can conserve resources.

You can also recycle the resources you do use.

Earth's Water

ESSENTIAL IDEA

Most of Earth's surface is covered with water.

Almost 75 percent of Earth's surface is covered with water. About 97 percent of that water is found in Earth's oceans. Ocean water is **salt water**. Another 2 percent of Earth's water is frozen in glaciers and ice caps.

ocean

About 3 percent of Earth's water is **freshwater**—water that you can use to drink or cook.

Rain is freshwater. When it rains, some water runs across Earth's surface. The water ends up in streams, rivers, and lakes. Most **rainwater** soaks into soil as **groundwater**.

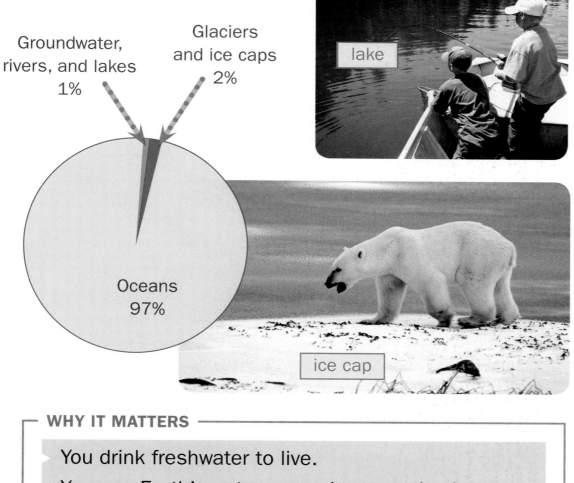

Groundwater, rivers, and lakes 1%

Glaciers and ice caps 2%

lake

Oceans 97%

ice cap

WHY IT MATTERS

You drink freshwater to live.

You use Earth's water every day to cook, clean, and play.

The Water Cycle

ESSENTIAL IDEA

> The water cycle is the movement of water from Earth's surface into the air and back to the surface again.

Earth's water constantly moves between the air and the surface.

This movement is called the **water cycle**.

1 **evaporation** The Sun heats water on Earth's surface. Water evaporates, or changes into a gas, and forms **water vapor**.

The water cycle includes **evaporation**, **condensation**, **precipitation**, and **collection**.

WHY IT MATTERS

> The water you use is part of the water cycle.

2 **condensation** Water vapor cools. It **condenses**, or changes into water, to form clouds.

3 **precipitation** Water falls back to Earth as precipitation. Rain and snow are types of precipitation.

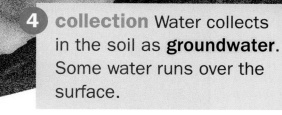

4 **collection** Water collects in the soil as **groundwater**. Some water runs over the surface.

Earth's Atmosphere

The gases that surround Earth form layers.

The gases that surround Earth are called the **atmosphere**. Gases in the atmosphere get thinner as you move away from Earth.

Earth's atmosphere has five main layers. The layers are the **exosphere**, **thermosphere**, **mesosphere**, **stratosphere**, and **troposphere**.

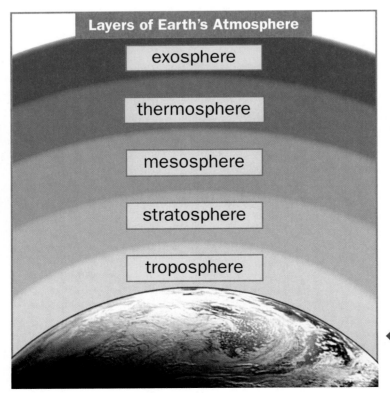

Layers of Earth's Atmosphere

exosphere

thermosphere

mesosphere

stratosphere

troposphere

◀ Nitrogen and oxygen are the main gases in Earth's atmosphere.

exosphere The exosphere is the farthest layer from Earth's surface.

thermosphere Temperature changes the most in the thermosphere.

mesosphere Meteors burn up when they enter the mesosphere.

stratosphere Jet planes fly near the bottom of the stratosphere.

troposphere The troposphere is the layer closest to Earth. Weather and clouds form in this layer.

WHY IT MATTERS

You breathe oxygen from the troposphere.
You live in the layer called the troposphere.

Air Masses

The way air masses move and interact causes weather.

An **air mass** is a large body of air with the same temperature. An air mass also has the same **humidity**, or amount of water vapor in it.

A **front** is the area where two air masses meet. When this happens, changes in weather can happen. It can start to rain or snow.

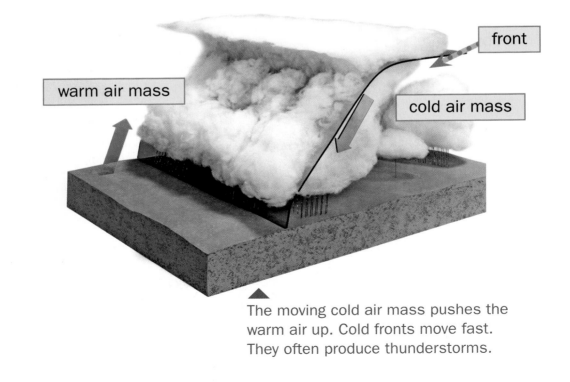

front

warm air mass

cold air mass

The moving cold air mass pushes the warm air up. Cold fronts move fast. They often produce thunderstorms.

High and Low Pressure

In air masses with high **pressure**, particles of gas are close together. Air masses with low pressure have particles that are farther apart. Differences in pressure cause **wind**.

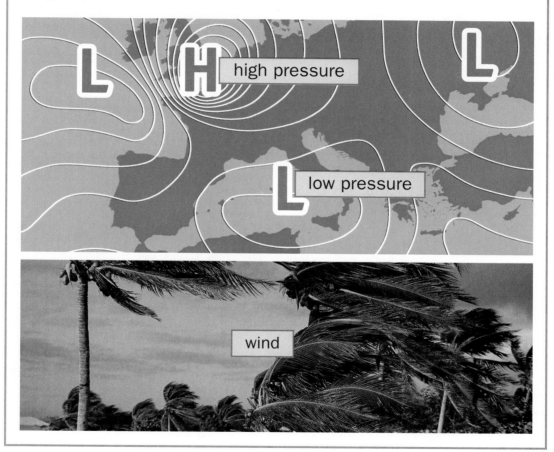

high pressure

low pressure

wind

WHY IT MATTERS

> You always have an air mass around you.
> The interaction of air masses causes changes in the weather around you.

Clouds

ESSENTIAL IDEA

Clouds are visible masses of tiny water drops or ice crystals. There are four basic types of clouds.

Clouds form when energy from the Sun causes water to evaporate from Earth's surface. As the water vapor rises, it cools to form tiny water drops or ice crystals. Clouds are a lot of tiny drops in one place.

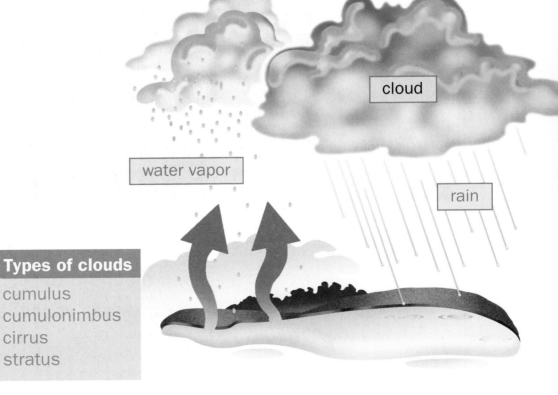

cloud

water vapor

rain

Types of clouds

cumulus
cumulonimbus
cirrus
stratus

Cumulus clouds are puffy, white clouds with flat bases.

Cumulonimbus clouds grow up and down. Big, dark clouds like these often bring rain.

Cirrus clouds are high, feathery clouds. They are made of ice crystals.

Stratus clouds are layers of clouds. These clouds don't bring much rain.

WHY IT MATTERS

You see different types of clouds.

You can use clouds to predict the weather.

Measuring Weather

ESSENTIAL IDEA

Tools help us measure different properties of weather.

Weather describes the outside conditions in a certain area. We use different tools to measure each of these conditions.

A **barometer** measures pressure in an air mass.

A **thermometer** measures temperature. Temperature is measured in degrees (°).

barometer

thermometer

The two main temperature scales are Fahrenheit (F) and Celsius (C). ▶

Measuring Wind

An **anemometer** measures wind speed. The wind makes the cups spin around. The faster the wind speed, the faster they spin.

A **wind vane** measures wind direction. The vane spins in the wind. The arrow points to the direction the wind is blowing.

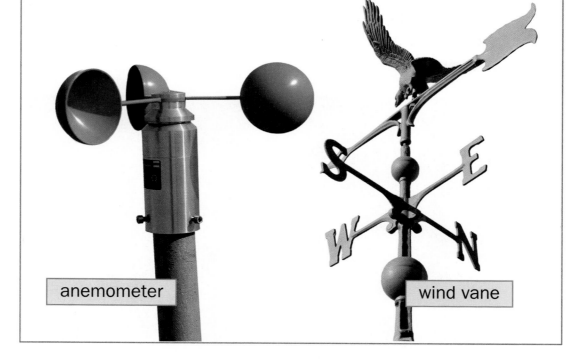

anemometer

wind vane

WHY IT MATTERS

Knowing the weather helps you decide what to wear.

You can use a thermometer to measure the temperature inside or outside.

Predicting Weather

┌─ **ESSENTIAL IDEA** ─────────────────

Meteorologists use tools to measure
weather conditions and predict the weather.

A weather **prediction** describes what the weather
will be like in the future. A prediction is also called
a **forecast**.

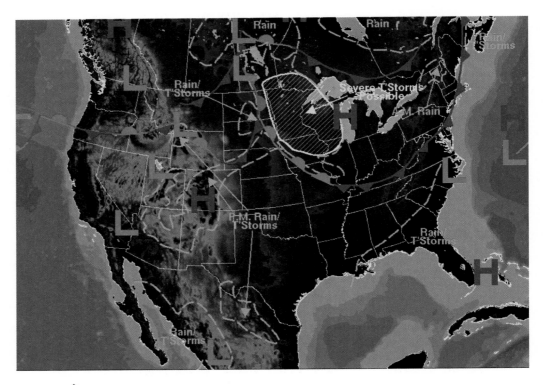

▲
Finding areas of high (H) and low (L) pressure helps to predict
where storms will hit.

A **meteorologist** is a person who studies and predicts weather. Meteorologists use pictures made from **radar** signals. The signals bounce off things like clouds and rain.

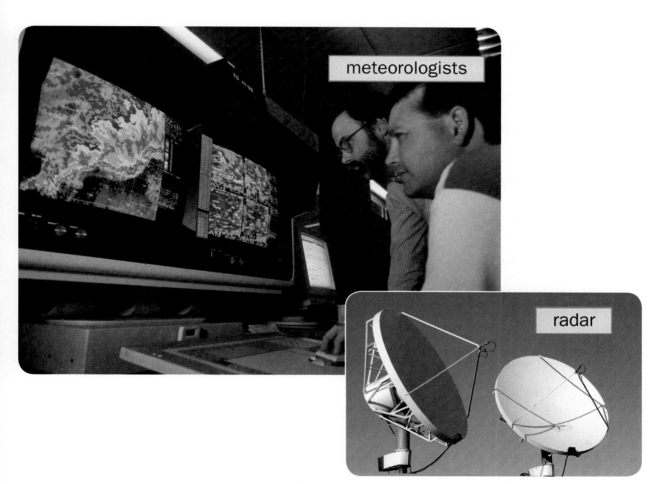

meteorologists

radar

WHY IT MATTERS

> You can use forecasts to make plans to do things outside.

> Meteorologists tell you the weather in your area.

Storms

The movement of air masses can cause severe weather.

Storms form when air masses meet at a front. A front is the boundary between warm and cold air masses.

How Storms Form

Warm air holds more water vapor than cold air. A cold front pushes the warm air up. Then the water vapor condenses. This forms clouds.

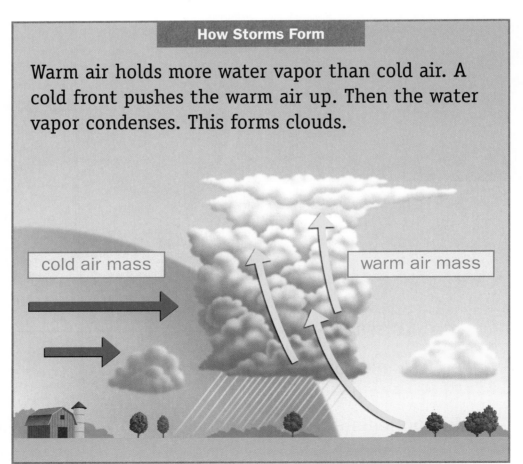

cold air mass

warm air mass

Thunderstorms

A **thunderstorm** is a strong storm with **lightning** and **thunder**.

Lightning is a giant spark in the sky. The spark heats the air. This causes the air to expand quickly. Thunder is the loud noise of the air expanding.

thunderstorm

lightning

Storms *continued*

Hurricanes

A **hurricane** is a large storm that forms over the ocean. Hurricanes can cause **damage**, or harm, when they move over land. Fast winds can bend and break trees.

The winds also cause huge waves. These **waves** damage buildings and boats.

waves

How a Hurricane Forms

Hurricanes only form where water temperatures stay warm for a long time.

1 The warm, humid ocean air rises.

2 More humid air rushes in to take its place.

3 The column of rising air begins to spin.

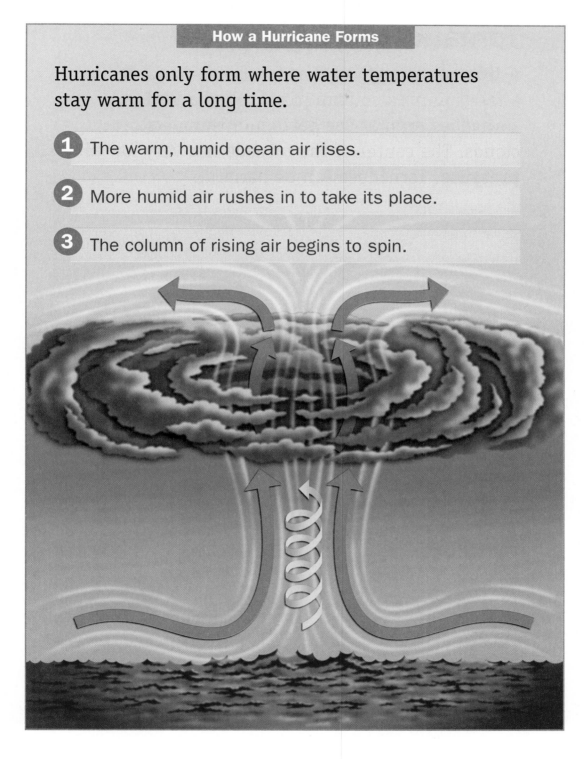

Tornadoes

A **tornado** is a storm that forms over land. It has a fast-spinning column of air called a **vortex**. Tornadoes form at the bottom of thunderstorm clouds. The center of the tornado has very low **air pressure**. Tornadoes can be harmful.

thunderstorm cloud

tornado

vortex

Some tornadoes move along the ground in a narrow path.

It can take several days to dig out after a blizzard ends.

Blizzards

A **blizzard** is a winter storm that has high winds and heavy, blowing snow. Blizzards form in cold weather and may last for several days.

WHY IT MATTERS

> You should know what to do when a storm comes.
> Where you live affects the kinds of storms you might get.

The Solar System

ESSENTIAL IDEA

The solar system includes the Sun and all objects that orbit it.

A **planet** is a large object that **orbits**, or moves around, the Sun. Eight planets orbit our Sun. The Sun and all the objects that orbit it are called a **solar system**.

solar system

Sun

Earth

planets

orbit

other galaxies

Milky Way galaxy

Our solar system is in the Milky Way galaxy. A
galaxy is a huge collection of stars, gas, and dust.
There are about 100 billion stars in a galaxy. The
universe has billions of galaxies.

WHY IT MATTERS

> You live on Earth, which is part of the solar system.
> Your solar system is part of the Milky Way galaxy.

Day and Night

Earth spins on its axis. This movement gives us day and night.

Earth has day and night because Earth **rotates**, or spins on its axis. The **axis** is an imaginary line running through the center of Earth. Earth's axis **slants**, or tilts.

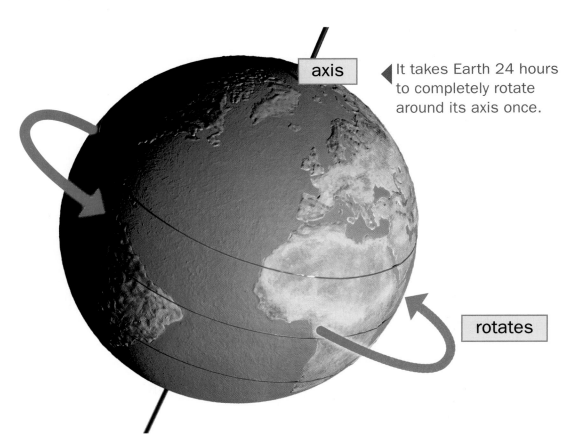

axis

It takes Earth 24 hours to completely rotate around its axis once.

rotates

How the Sun Lights Earth

The Sun is the source of light on Earth. It is day for the part of Earth that is facing the Sun. It is night for the part of Earth facing away from the Sun.

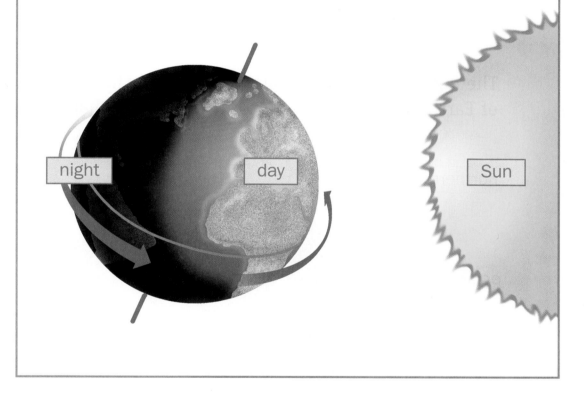

night

day

Sun

WHY IT MATTERS

When Earth is facing the Sun where you live it is day.

When Earth is facing away from the Sun where you live it is night.

Seasons

ESSENTIAL IDEA

Earth moves around the Sun in an orbit.
The tilt of Earth's axis causes seasons.

The **equator** is an imaginary line around the middle of Earth. The equator divides Earth into two halves.

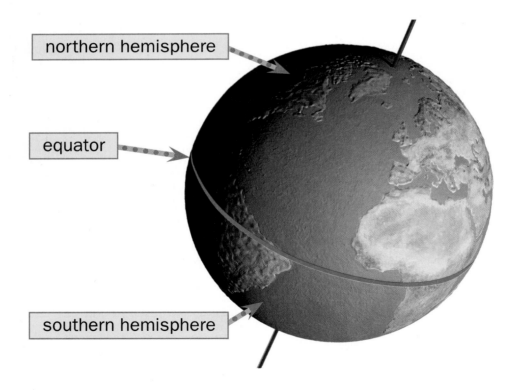

northern hemisphere

equator

southern hemisphere

▲
The half of Earth north of the equator is the northern hemisphere.
The half south of the equator is the southern hemisphere.

Earth **revolves**, or moves, around the Sun. One **revolution** takes a year. When Earth's axis tilts towards the Sun, the northern **hemisphere** gets more direct sunlight in the summer.

The northern hemisphere has winter when Earth's axis tilts away from the Sun.

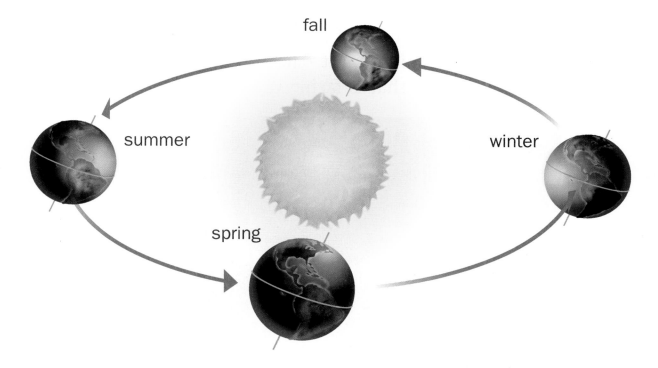

WHY IT MATTERS

You feel warmer in summer because the Sun's rays strike you more directly than in winter.

149

The Moon

ESSENTIAL IDEA

The Moon gives off no light of its own.

The **Moon** has no light of its own. We see it because the Sun's light shines on it. The Sun lights only the side of the Moon that is facing it.

Moon

◀ The lighted part of the Moon we see from Earth depends on the positions of Earth, the Moon, and the Sun.

How the Moon Changes

The Moon goes around Earth about once each month. Even though the Moon is always lighted the same by the Sun, the lighted part we can see from Earth changes as the Moon revolves. These changes are called **phases** of the Moon.

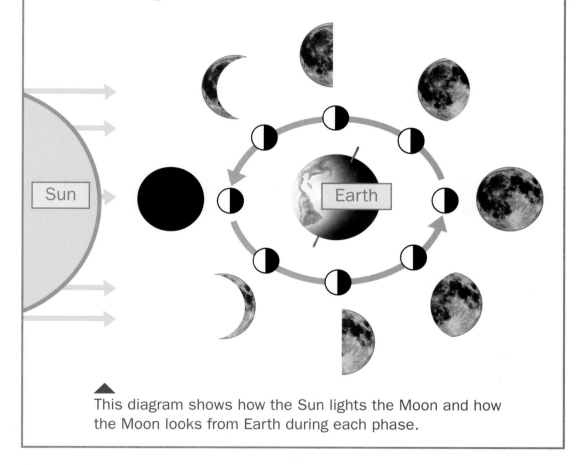

▲ This diagram shows how the Sun lights the Moon and how the Moon looks from Earth during each phase.

WHY IT MATTERS

You may be able to see all the phases of the Moon about once a month.

Other Objects in Space

ESSENTIAL IDEA

Smaller objects are also found in space.

The Sun, planets, and moons are the largest bodies in the solar system. **Space** also contains many smaller objects.

A **meteor** is a piece of rock from space that burns up as it enters our atmosphere.

A **meteorite** is a piece of rock from space that lands on Earth.

Meteorites landing on Earth can form craters, such as this one in Arizona.

crater

An **asteroid** is a small rocky body that orbits a **star.**

asteroid

A **comet** is a chunk of ice and dust. It orbits the Sun. The comet forms a tail of ice particles and dust as it moves.

comet

WHY IT MATTERS

Objects from space can hit Earth and cause damage.

153

What Is Matter?

ESSENTIAL IDEA

Matter is anything that takes up space.

Matter makes up everything around you. Air, a glass of water, a chair—anything that takes up space is matter. Even you are made of matter.

▲ Everything in this picture is made of matter.

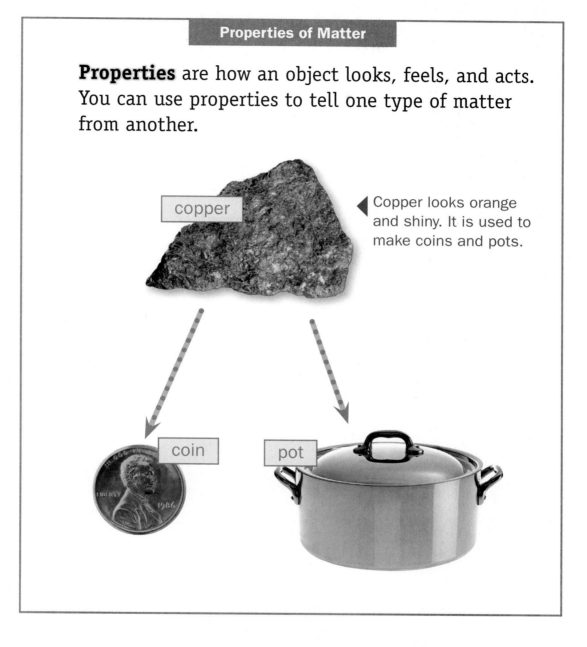

Properties of Matter

Properties are how an object looks, feels, and acts. You can use properties to tell one type of matter from another.

copper

Copper looks orange and shiny. It is used to make coins and pots.

coin

pot

WHY IT MATTERS

You are made of matter.

Everything you touch and use is made of matter.

States of Matter

ESSENTIAL IDEA

Matter exists in three different states.

Matter can exist in three different **states**, or forms. You can observe matter as a **solid**, **liquid**, or **gas**.

▲ This picture shows water in all three states. The snow is a solid. Steam, or water vapor, is a gas. Steam rises above a pool of warm water—a liquid.

How Matter Changes

Matter changes from one state to another when it is heated or cooled.

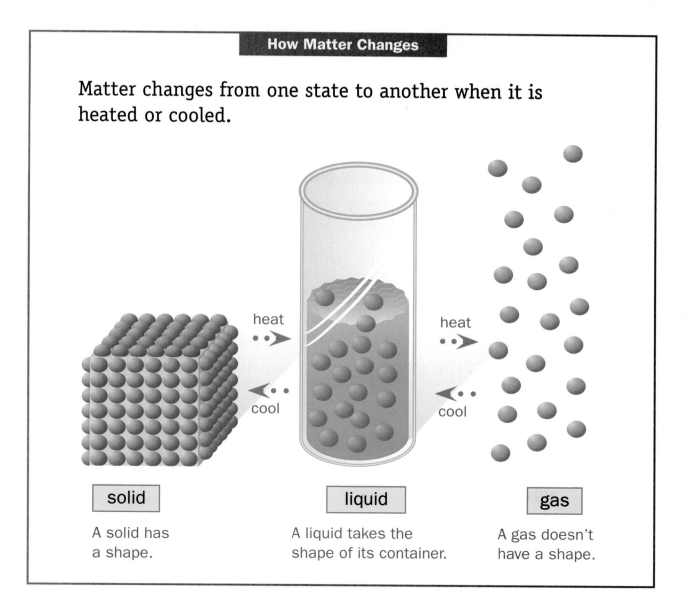

solid	liquid	gas
A solid has a shape.	A liquid takes the shape of its container.	A gas doesn't have a shape.

WHY IT MATTERS

The air around you is a gas.

You drink liquids and use water to wash yourself.

The floor you walk on and the chairs you sit on are solid.

Measuring Matter

ESSENTIAL IDEA

Scientists use tools to measure the mass and volume of matter.

You can measure many properties of matter.

Mass

Mass is the amount of matter in an object. A unit of mass is the **gram** (g). You measure mass using a **balance**.

▼ The grams are used to measure the mass of the tomatoes.

grams

balance

Volume

Volume is the amount of space an object takes up. A unit of volume is a **liter** (L). You can use a **measuring cup** to measure liquids.

▲
A liquid will keep the same volume in different containers.

measuring cup

Density

Density is the amount of mass of a certain volume of an object. Two objects can have the same volume but different masses. You have to compare equal volumes of both kinds of matter to compare the density of each object.

bowling ball

soccer ball

The mass of the bowling ball is much greater than the mass of the soccer ball.

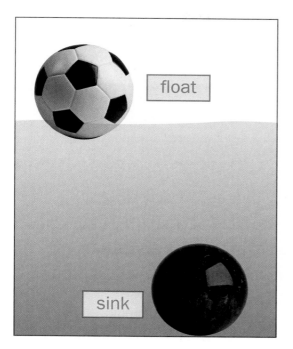

float

sink

The soccer ball and bowling ball have the same volume. But the bowling ball feels heavier. The bowling ball has more mass. That's what makes the soccer ball float and the bowling ball sink.

measurements	definition
mass	amount of matter in an object
volume	amount of space an object takes up
density	amount of mass of a certain volume of an object

WHY IT MATTERS

Your mass is the amount of matter in your body.

Your volume is the amount of space you take up.

You may have seen some objects float on water because they have a low density.

Atoms and Elements

ESSENTIAL IDEA

Atoms make up all matter.

All matter is made of tiny pieces, or **particles**. An **atom** is the smallest particle of matter that has the properties of that matter. A **substance**, or matter, made of only one kind of atom is called an **element**.

Metal elements
nickel
iron
silver
aluminum
copper
gold

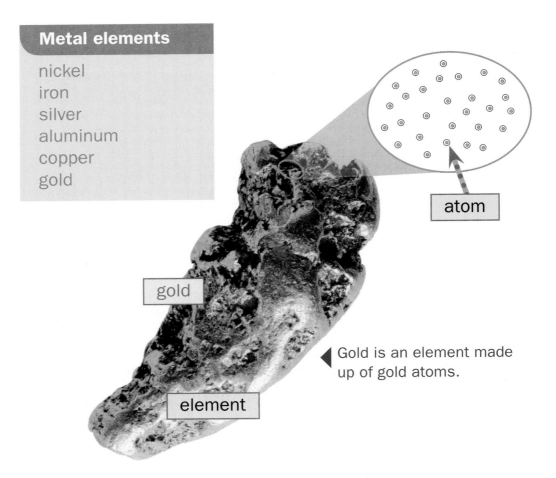

atom

gold

element

Gold is an element made up of gold atoms.

Most substances are made up of different types of particles.

- ▲ minerals
- ⬭ air
- ● water
- ■ other

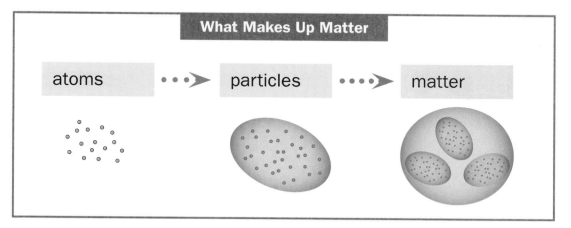

WHY IT MATTERS

> You are made of atoms.

> All matter around you is made of elements.

Physical Changes in Matter

ESSENTIAL IDEA

A physical change does not change the particles that make up matter.

When making ice cubes from water, the water is **freezing**, or changing to a solid. If ice cubes are **melting**, they are changing back to a liquid.

Freezing and melting are **physical changes**. **Boiling** is a physical change from liquid to gas.

ice cubes

melting

boiling

If you add salt to water, the salt seems to disappear. The salt **dissolves** in the water to form a **solution**. A solution is a mixture that looks like one substance.

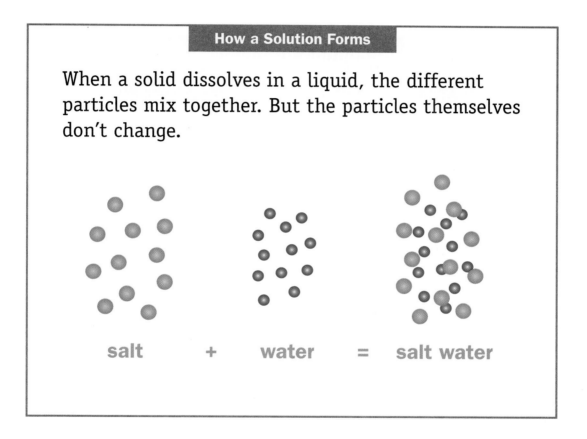

How a Solution Forms

When a solid dissolves in a liquid, the different particles mix together. But the particles themselves don't change.

salt   +   water   =   salt water

WHY IT MATTERS

> You see physical changes, like making ice, every day.

> You use solutions, like soapy water, in daily life.

Chemical Changes in Matter

ESSENTIAL IDEA

A chemical change produces a completely different form of matter.

Making a fire changes wood into ashes. The black part on the wood is a new substance. **Burning** is a chemical change. A **chemical change** is one that produces one or more new forms of matter.

burning

Rusting is a chemical change. When rust forms on a car, you can't wash it off. The metal in the car has changed to something else.

rusting

Signs of chemical change

color or other properties change

bubbles appear or a new solid forms

can't get back what was started with

WHY IT MATTERS

Cooking your food is a chemical change.

169

Energy

Energy is needed to move or change things.

Every day you see things moving all around you. **Energy** is the ability to move or change things.

The Sun is Earth's main source of energy. The Sun's energy is **stored** in food and fossil fuels. Stored energy is called **potential energy**.

This car uses the stored energy in fossil fuels, such as gasoline, to move fast. Objects in motion have **kinetic energy**.

WHY IT MATTERS

When you eat, you are giving your body energy.
Without energy, you couldn't move or play.

Heat Energy

Heat energy is energy that moves between things at different temperatures.

Rubbing your hands together creates **heat energy**. The heat energy warms up your hands. Moving **particles** of matter have heat energy.

When you rub your hands together, the energy of your motion changes to heat energy.

heat energy

Temperature

Temperature is a measure of how fast the particles are moving in a substance. When a substance is heated, the particles speed up.

WHY IT MATTERS

> You use heat energy when you cook, warm a room, or rub your hands together.

How Heat Moves

ESSENTIAL IDEA

Heat energy moves from one place to another in three main ways.

Heat energy can move in different ways.

Conduction

When particles of matter bump into one another, energy moves from one particle to another. This is called **conduction**.

Energy moves quickly in some substances, like metals. These substances are called **conductors**.

The metal pan is a conductor. ▶

metal pan

Convection

Particles in liquids and gases do not stay in one place like they do in solids. As they move, they carry heat energy. This is called **convection**.

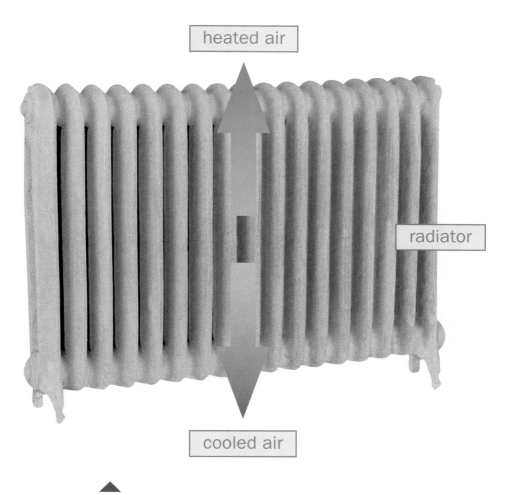

heated air

radiator

cooled air

▲ The heated air from a radiator rises to the ceiling. The cooled air moves down to the floor.

PHYSICAL SCIENCE

Radiation

Radiation is the movement of energy through space without using particles. Some matter **absorbs**, or takes in, energy easily. Shiny surfaces cause energy to bounce back, or **reflect**.

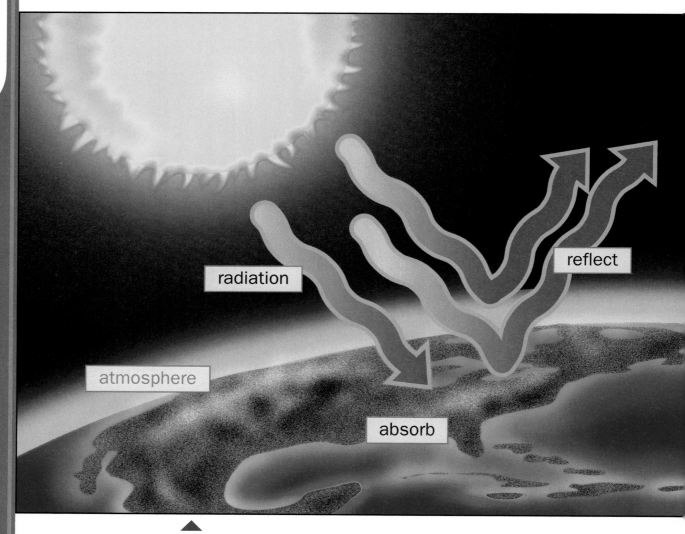

radiation

reflect

atmosphere

absorb

▲
The Sun's energy heats Earth's surface.

How Heat Moves

Heat energy moves from one place to another by conduction, convection, and radiation.

conduction

convection

radiation

WHY IT MATTERS

When you heat something, the heat energy is moving.

You wear light colored clothing in the summer to reflect the Sun's energy.

Static Electricity

ESSENTIAL IDEA

Static electricity involves the movement of electric charges from one place to another.

All matter contains **positive** (+) and **negative** (−) **charges**. Most matter has an equal number of positive and negative charges.

Sometimes negative charges build up on one surface and jump to another surface all at once. This movement is called **static electricity**.

Lightning is a form of static electricity. Charges build up on the clouds. Then they jump to the ground in a huge spark.

Like, or the same, electric charges **repel** one another. Unlike, or opposite, electric charges **attract** one another.

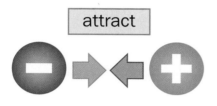

unlike charges attract

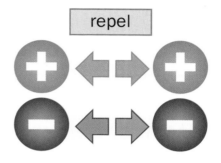

like charges repel

The negative charge on the balloon attracts the positive charge of the hair.

WHY IT MATTERS

You may have felt a shock from static electricity.

You use static electricity to watch television and turn on the lights.

179

Current Electricity

ESSENTIAL IDEA

A circuit is a path through which an electric current can flow.

Electricity is a form of energy. It involves the **flow**, or movement, of electric **charges**.

The flow of charges through a **circuit** is called an electric **current**.

In a circuit, electric current flows through metal wires. Electric circuits are made of metals such as copper or aluminum. Such metals are **conductors**.

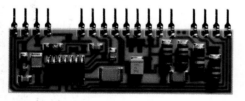

▲
A circuit like this is in remote controllers.

How Current Electricity Flows

An electric current flows through this closed circuit. A closed circuit is not broken. The charges pass from the battery through a metal wire to the light bulb. The wire in the light bulb gets hot and gives off light.

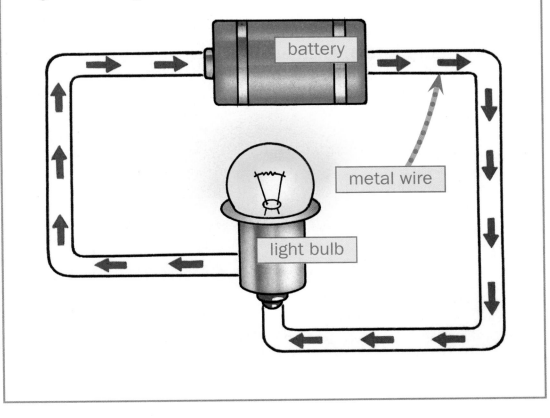

battery

metal wire

light bulb

WHY IT MATTERS

You use an electric current when you turn lights on.

Magnets

ESSENTIAL IDEA

A magnet attracts certain metals.

A **magnet** is an object or material that attracts certain **metals**, such as iron.

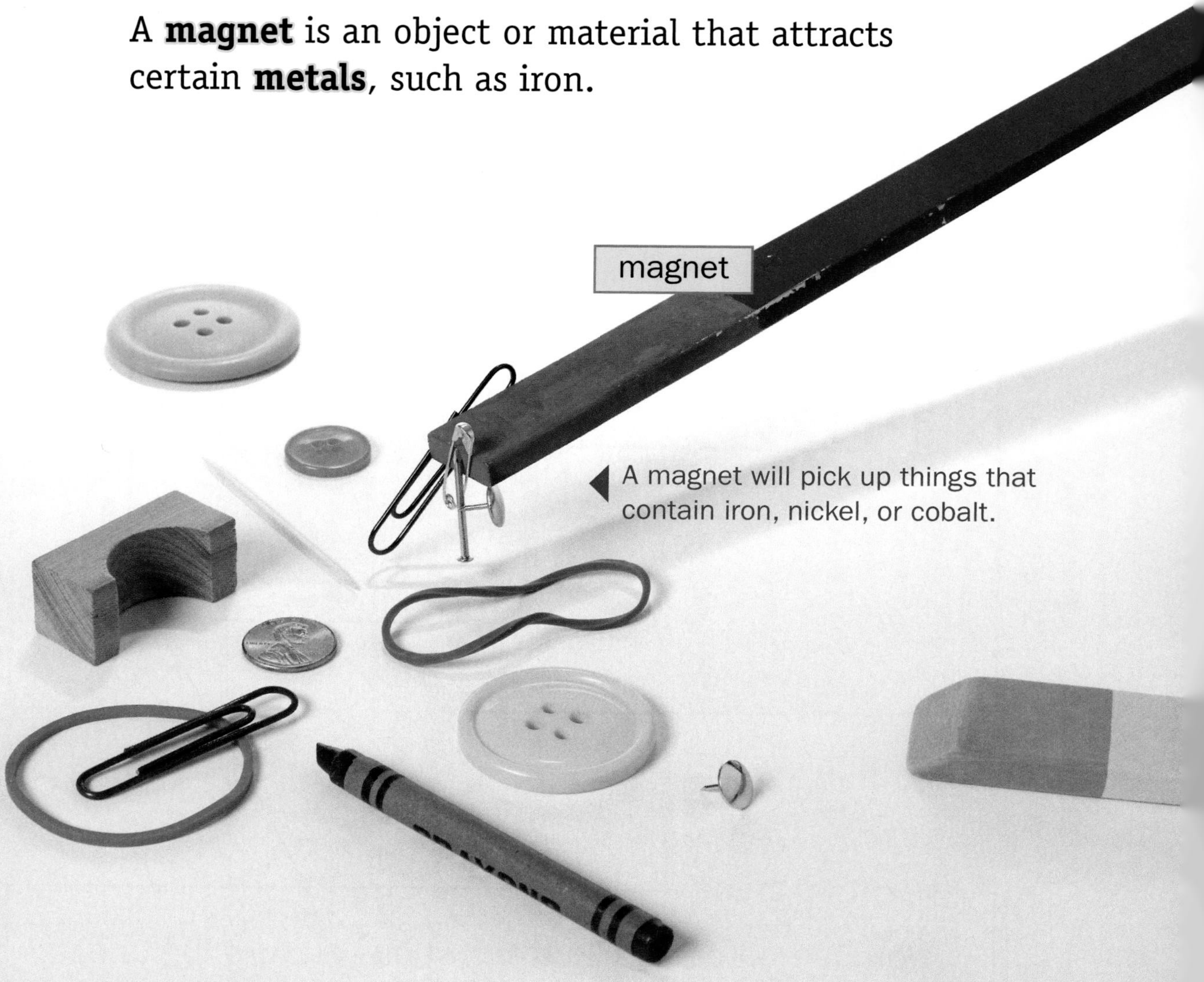

magnet

◄ A magnet will pick up things that contain iron, nickel, or cobalt.

The needle on the **compass** is a magnet. Its south pole points to Earth's north pole because opposite poles attract.

compass

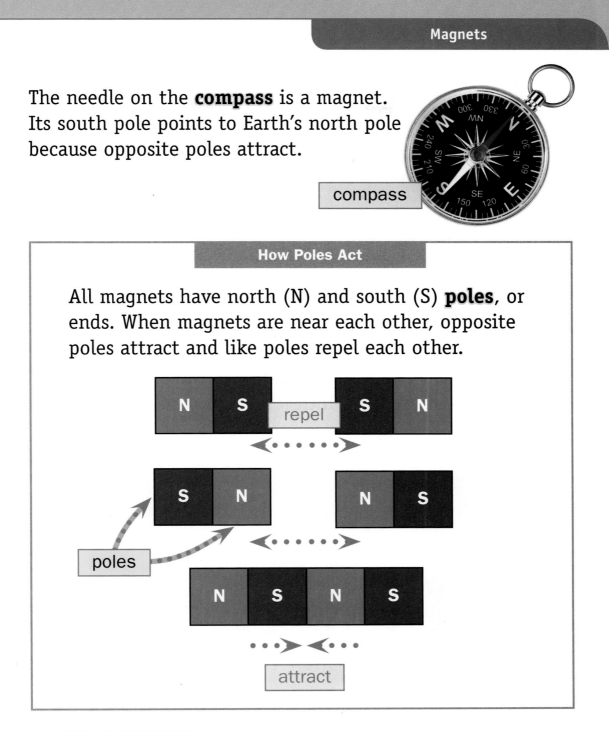

How Poles Act

All magnets have north (N) and south (S) **poles**, or ends. When magnets are near each other, opposite poles attract and like poles repel each other.

repel

poles

attract

WHY IT MATTERS

> A magnet in a compass helps you figure out which direction is North, South, West, and East.

Sound

Sound is a form of energy that you can hear.

Musical instruments make air **vibrate**, or move back and forth. The vibrations create a **wave**. The wave travels through air until it reaches your ear.

▲

The energy in a sound wave makes your eardrum vibrate. You hear the sound each instrument makes.

What Makes an Echo

When you make a sound, some waves can bounce off hard surfaces. You hear an **echo** when the waves come back to your ear.

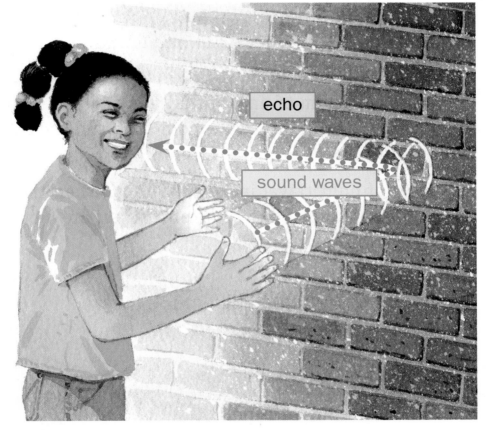

echo

sound waves

The sound of the girl clapping makes an echo.

WHY IT MATTERS

> You make sounds when you speak.
> You hear a sound when sound waves reach your eardrum.

Light Energy

ESSENTIAL IDEA

Light behaves in different ways when it strikes matter.

Light is a form of energy that you can see. Light energy moves in waves. A light bulb and the Sun are both **sources** of light.

Rays of light travel in straight lines. When the light hits something, some of the rays are blocked. This creates a **shadow**.

The Sun's rays are blocked and make shadows.

shadow

You see most objects because light **reflects**, or bounces off of them.

Reflection of Light

When you look in a mirror, light rays bounce off the smooth mirror. All the reflected rays bounce back in the same way. This forms a clear **image.**

◀ Light rays reflected from a smooth surface.

▲ Smooth water is like a mirror. The reflection is clear.

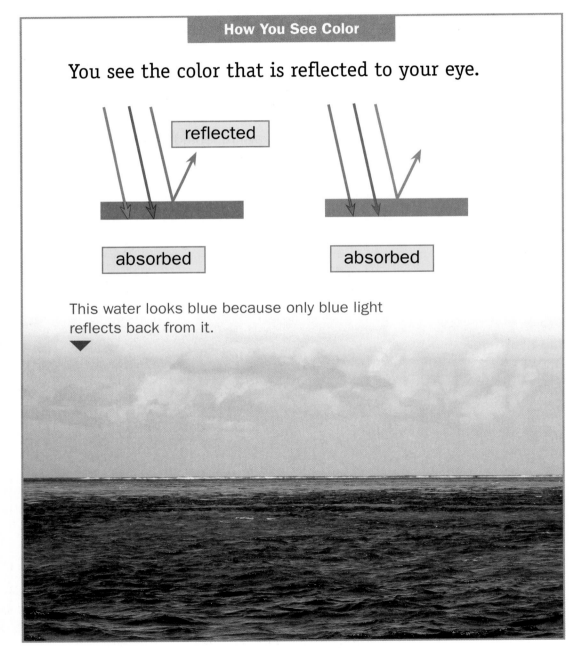

Color

The Sun's light contains all **colors**. Some objects **absorb**, or take in, certain colors and **reflect** other ones.

How You See Color

You see the color that is reflected to your eye.

reflected

absorbed

absorbed

This water looks blue because only blue light reflects back from it.

Refraction

Light moves through clear substances, like glass and water. When this happens, the light rays sometimes **refract**, or change direction.

refract

▲ Refraction makes this pen look broken.

Lenses are curved pieces of glass that refract light.

lens

▲ This lens uses refraction to make objects look bigger.

┌─ **WHY IT MATTERS** ─────────────

▌ Colors are absorbed and reflected all around you.

Motion

ESSENTIAL IDEA

An object is in motion when it changes its position.

Something is moving when it changes its **position**. **Motion** is a change of position. An object at rest isn't moving.

motion

position 1

position 2

Measuring Speed

Some things move very slowly, and others move too fast to see. **Speed** is a measure of how quickly an object changes position. Speed equals **distance** divided by **time**.

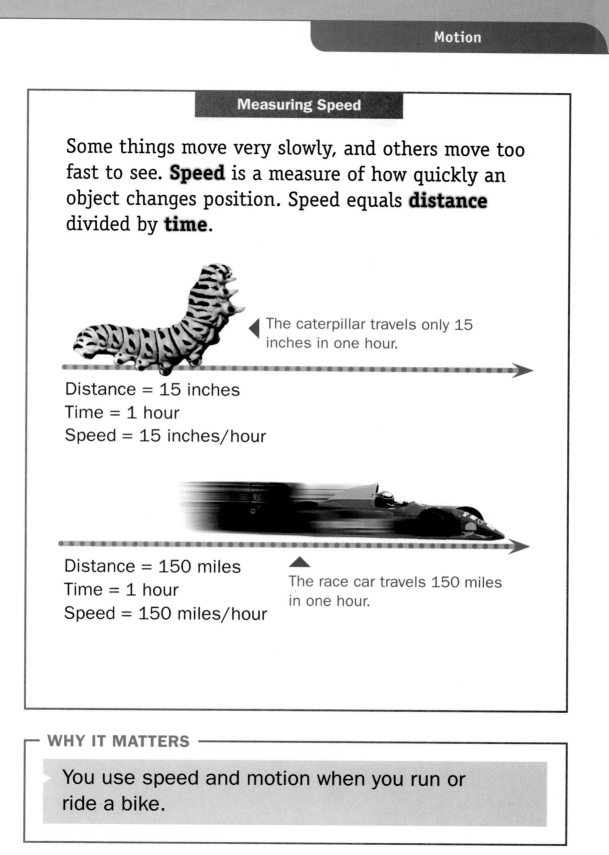

The caterpillar travels only 15 inches in one hour.

Distance = 15 inches
Time = 1 hour
Speed = 15 inches/hour

The race car travels 150 miles in one hour.

Distance = 150 miles
Time = 1 hour
Speed = 150 miles/hour

WHY IT MATTERS

You use speed and motion when you run or ride a bike.

Force

ESSENTIAL IDEA

A force is a push or pull on an object.

A **force** acts on an object to make it move, stop, or change **direction**.

▼ The bat pushes the ball with so much force that the ball changes its shape. The bat can also change the ball's direction and speed.

force

Friction is a force that happens when two things rub against each other. There is much more friction on a rough surface than on a smooth surface.

friction

▲
Friction keeps you from sliding around on surfaces when you ride a bike.

WHY IT MATTERS

> You use forces to move objects.
> You use the force of friction to stop your bike.

193

Gravity

Gravity is a force that pulls objects toward each other.

Gravity is a **force** that pulls objects toward each other.

The force of gravity depends on the mass of the objects pulling toward each other. It also depends on the distance between the objects.

The skydiver falls quickly toward Earth.

The astronaut is far from Earth so the force of gravity is smaller. She appears to float.

Weight is a measure of the force of gravity on an object. On Earth, the more mass an object has, the more it weighs.

▲
The astronaut has the same mass on Earth and in space. But the astronaut's weight is less in space because the force of gravity is smaller.

WHY IT MATTERS

▶ Gravity holds you on Earth's surface.

Simple Machines

ESSENTIAL IDEA

Simple machines help us do work.

You do **work** when you apply a force to an object, and the object moves. A **machine** is a tool that makes work easier.

A ramp is simple machine called an **inclined plane**.

The **wheel and axle** is a simple machine. It reduces friction to make work easier.

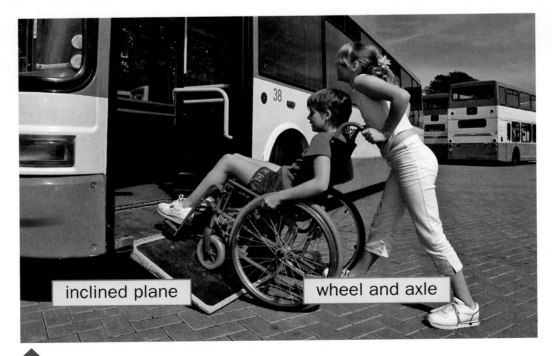

inclined plane

wheel and axle

▲
The ramp helps the wheel chair move with less force.

A **screw** is an inclined plane wrapped around a tube. A screwdriver makes it easier to push a metal screw into the wood.

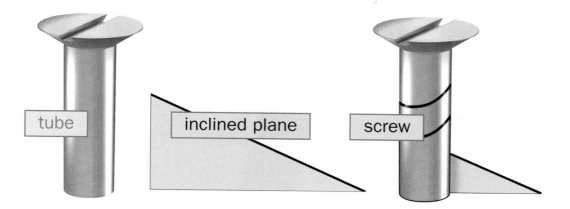

tube

inclined plane

screw

A **wedge** is an inclined plane turned on edge. You use a wedge to break things apart. A knife is a wedge used to break food apart.

The front of this kayak is shaped like a wedge. This helps it move through the water more easily.

wedge

People often use levers to move heavy objects. A **lever** is a bar that turns around a point that doesn't move. The fixed point is called the **fulcrum**. When you push or pull on a lever, it causes the bar to turn around the fulcrum. The other end of the bar moves.

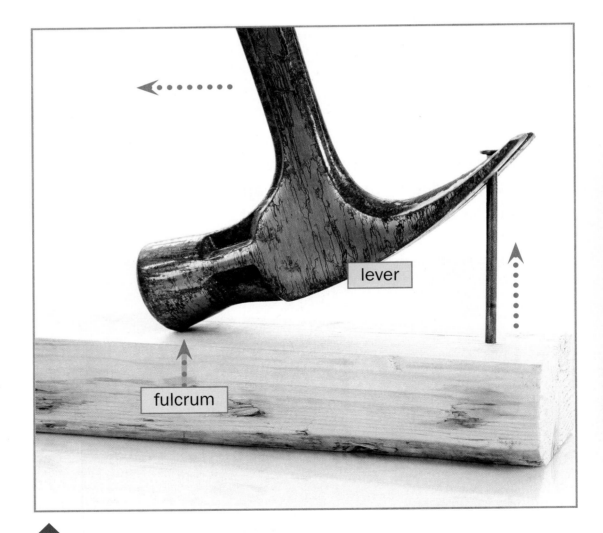

lever

fulcrum

▲
A lever makes it easy to pull the nail out of the wood.

A **pulley** is another simple machine. It has a wheel and axle and a rope. A single pulley changes the direction of the force. Instead of lifting up, you can pull down.

How a Pulley Works

pulley

When you pull on the rope of a pulley, the wheel turns around the axle. This force lets you move things up and down.

WHY IT MATTERS

You use simple machines to help you do work.

Technology

ESSENTIAL IDEA

Technology is applying knowledge of science to make life easier.

Scientists **apply**, or use, ideas to make useful tools. This is called **technology**.

Computers are an example of technology. These tools were built with help from scientists.

▲
Early computers were bigger than a refrigerator. Now computers can fit on a fingertip.

Technology can make **transportation** devices to move you from place to place.

▼ This train runs on magnets and floats just above the track.

▲
Someday, you might fly your own personal airplane to work.

WHY IT MATTERS

You use technology every day.

Technology will make your life easier in the future.

Studying Science

Science Process Skills

ESSENTIAL IDEA

Scientists use skills to help them find answers to questions.

Science is about asking **questions** and finding **answers** to the questions.

▲ These scientists are using science process skills.

Scientists use a **process**, or a number of steps, to answer questions. Each of the steps uses a **skill**, or ability. The steps can happen in any order. Scientists often repeat steps before they find an answer.

◀ Scientists can use their sense of sight to observe a plant fossil.

Science Process Skills	
skill	**meaning**
observe	use senses to notice
classify	put in groups
estimate and measure	find amount of something
predict	say what will happen
infer	make a conclusion using information
communicate	share information

STUDYING SCIENCE

Observing

When you observe, you use your senses to get information about objects and events.

Objects have **properties** like color, size, shape, or the way they feel. You **observe** the properties with your **senses**.

chimpanzees

▲ Jane Goodall, a famous scientist, is observing the chimpanzees' behavior.

Using Your Senses

Your senses include sight, hearing, taste, touch, and smell.

	sense	description
	sight	I use my eyes to see.
	hearing	I use my ears to hear.
	taste	I use my mouth to taste.
	touch	I use my hands to touch.
	smell	I use my nose to smell.

I see the white petals.

The petals feel soft.

petals

STUDYING SCIENCE

Classifying

You **classify** objects when you put them into groups. Scientists classify objects by their **properties**. Properties describe things and events.

All the objects in a group are **alike**, or the same, in some way. Objects with **different** properties go in other groups.

▲
The shapes of some of the shells are alike. Some shells are different colors.

There are many ways to classify objects. For example, you can classify objects by size, shape, and color.

Ways to Classify Objects

size	shape	color

These shells are the same size.

These shells are alike. They are round.

These shells are red.

Estimating and Measuring

To **estimate** is to make a **reasonable** answer based on what you know. You might estimate the weight or length of an object. You use a tool to find out if your estimate is correct.

I estimate this fish weighs about four pounds.

You **measure** the **exact** amount of a property using units. **Units** are amounts that everyone agrees to.

You use tools to measure objects. The units are marked on the tool.

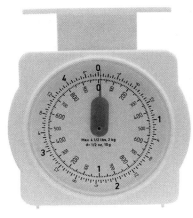

▲ A scale measures the weight of an object.

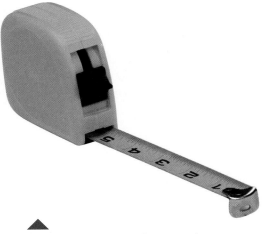

▲ A tape measure is a tool for measuring length.

Lab Report

Estimates

    Length: _18 inches_____

    Weight: _4 pounds_____

Measurements

    Length: _____20_____ inches

    Weight: _____5_____ pounds

Predicting

To **predict** is to say what you think will happen next. Scientists use **knowledge** or information that they observe to make a **prediction**.

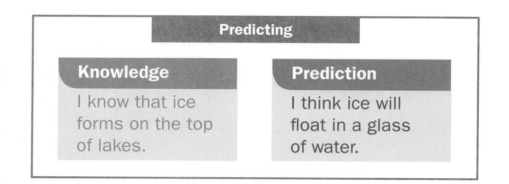

Predicting	
Knowledge	**Prediction**
I know that ice forms on the top of lakes.	I think ice will float in a glass of water.

Does ice sink or float in water?

Testing a Prediction

1 Put water in a glass.

2 Place ice cubes in water.

3 Observe what happens.

4 Check your prediction.

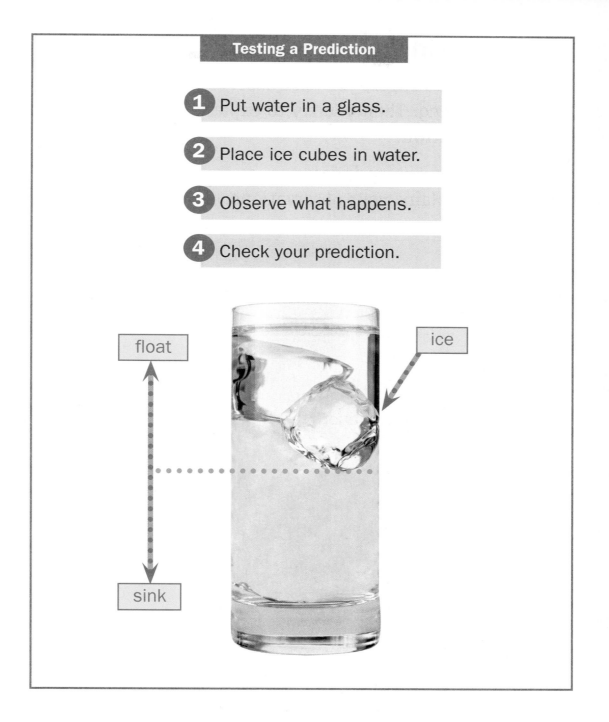

float

sink

ice

STUDYING SCIENCE

Inferring

When you **infer**, you first observe what is happening. Then you try to explain your **observation**.

Finally, make an **inference**, or conclusion, that explains your observations.

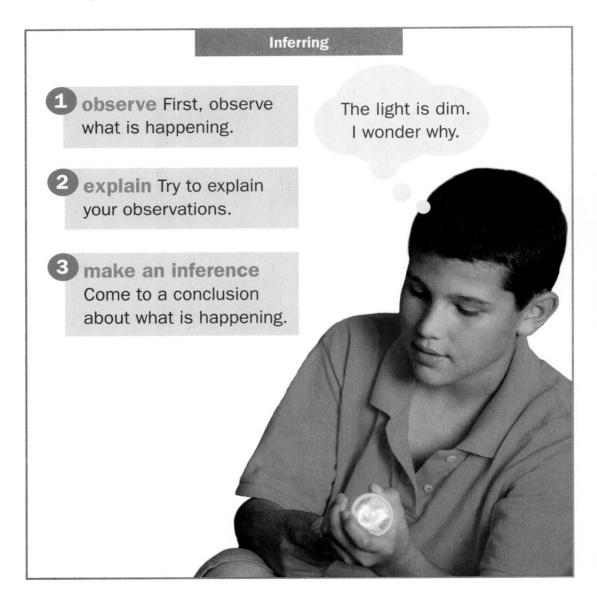

Inferring

1 **observe** First, observe what is happening.

2 **explain** Try to explain your observations.

3 **make an inference** Come to a conclusion about what is happening.

The light is dim. I wonder why.

How to Infer

1 **Observe what is happening.** | The light is dim.

2 **Try to explain your observations.** | This happened last time I left the flashlight on too long.

3 **Make an inference.** | The flashlight needs new batteries.

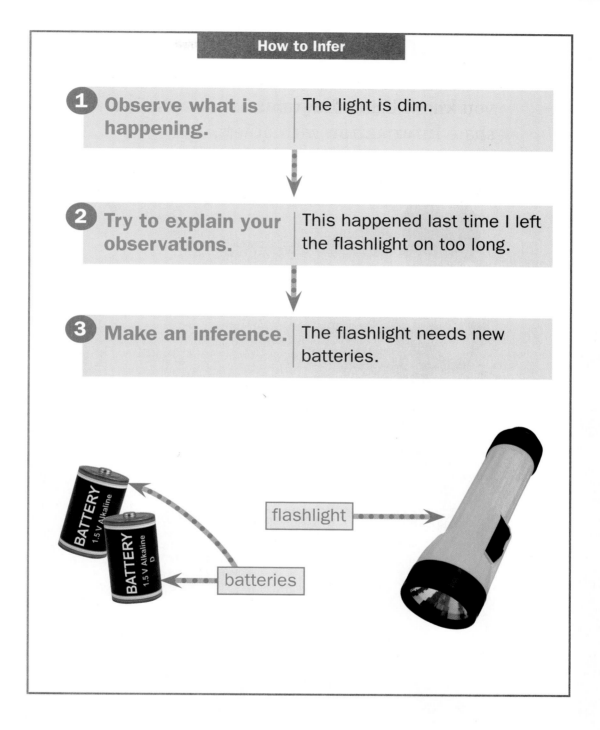

Communicating

You use words and pictures to **communicate** what you know. Using **diagrams** and **graphs** is a way to share **information** with others.

information

The boy is communicating information about a volcano to the class.

A diagram shows information with a picture.

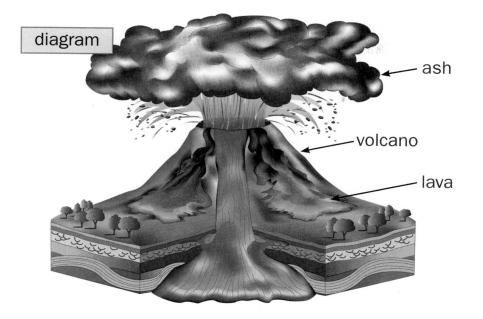

diagram

← ash

volcano

lava

A graph is one way to compare information.

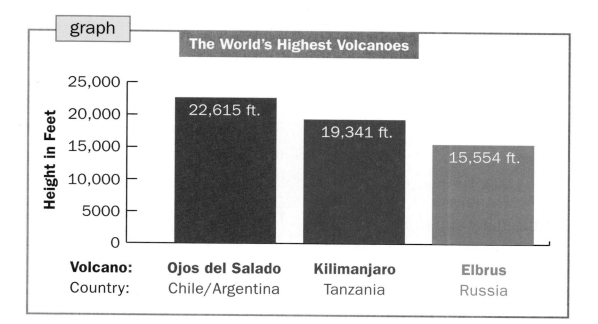

graph

The World's Highest Volcanoes

22,615 ft.	19,341 ft.	15,554 ft.

Height in Feet: 25,000 / 20,000 / 15,000 / 10,000 / 5000 / 0

Volcano:	Ojos del Salado	Kilimanjaro	Elbrus
Country:	Chile/Argentina	Tanzania	Russia

Using Scientific Methods

Scientists use scientific methods to help them solve problems.

A **method** is a plan of action. You decide what steps to do and in what order to do them. Scientists always use a series of steps to **solve** problems. The series of steps is called a **scientific method**.

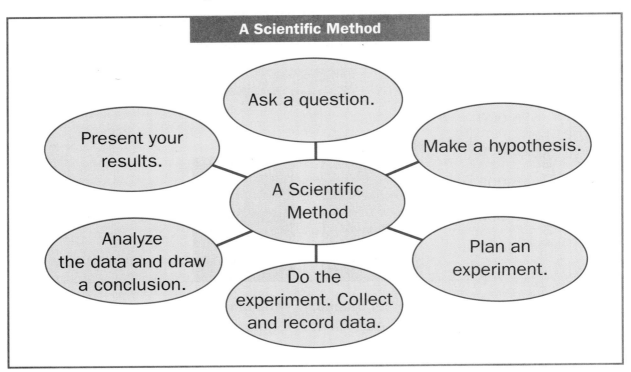

A Scientific Method

- Ask a question.
- Make a hypothesis.
- A Scientific Method
- Present your results.
- Plan an experiment.
- Analyze the data and draw a conclusion.
- Do the experiment. Collect and record data.

Here are the steps for an experiment:

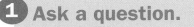 **Ask a question.**

Ask a question about something you observe.
You might ask, "Why don't plants grow well near
smoke stacks?"

2 Make a hypothesis.

Tell what you think is a possible answer to your
question. The possible answer is your **hypothesis**.

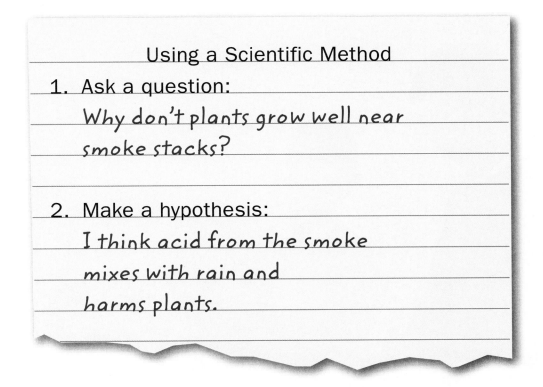

3 **Plan an experiment to test your hypothesis. Control the variables.**

Once you have your hypothesis, plan a way to test it. A scientific test is called an **experiment**. You can test if acid rain is harmful by watering plants with vinegar and water. Vinegar is an acid.

3. Plan an experiment:
   I will water some plants with water.
   I will water some with vinegar and water.
   I will see which plants grow better.

A **variable** is something that can change. In this experiment, the amount of vinegar in the water is the variable you will test.

Variable to Test:

    Four plants will get plain water. Four plants will get vinegar and water.

Controlled Variables:

☑ Same type of plants
☑ Same amount of sunlight

You must control all the possible variables, except the one you are testing. All of the other variables must be the same. For example, the amount of sunlight each plant gets must be the same.

STUDYING SCIENCE

4 **Do the experiment. Collect and record data.**

Data is information about the variable you are testing. **Collecting data** means making observations and measurements. **Record**, or write down, everything you observe.

Record your data in a chart or table. This makes the data easier to read and understand.

Be sure to label your plants so you don't get them mixed up.

Data Collection:

Day	Data
1	All the plants look green and healthy.
2	The leaves on the plants with vinegar and water look droopy.
3	The plants with plain water look green. The plants with vinegar and water look yellow.
4	Most of the plants with vinegar and water have lost their color.

STUDYING SCIENCE

5 Analyze the data and draw a conclusion.

To **analyze** data means to think about what the facts mean. Then you make a **conclusion**. This means you decide whether your hypothesis was right or wrong. That is the **result** of your experiment.

Scientists may create another experiment if the hypothesis was wrong.

6 Present your results.

Share what you have learned with others. You might write a **report** about your experiment.

report

Acid rain
harms
plant

Summary

1. Ask a question:

   Why don't plants grow well near smoke stacks?

2. Make a hypothesis:

   I think acid from the smoke mixes with rain and harms plants.

3. Plan an experiment:

   I will water some plants with water. I will water some with vinegar and water. I will see which plants grow better.

4. Do the experiment:

   Collect and record data.

Data collection

Day	Data
1	All the plants look green and healthy.
2	The leaves on the plants with vinegar and water look droopy.
3	The plants with water look green. The plants with vinegar and water look yellow.
4	Most of the plants with vinegar and water have lost their color.

5. Analyze the data and draw a conclusion:

   The vinegar and water made the plants worse every day. Acid rain does harm plants.

┌─ **WHY IT MATTERS** ─────────────────

You can answer questions using scientific methods.

Part Two

Literacy Essentials

This part of the book will help you read and write about science.

Reading Science

Science Textbooks

ESSENTIAL IDEA

Information is organized in science textbooks so that you can understand it easily.

Topics are grouped in textbooks into **units**. Units name big topics, like Life Science. **Chapters** in the unit tell more about smaller topics.

unit

chapters

UNIT 1 Energy and Food

How do organisms get energy?

Producers
Consumers
Decomposers

Chapter 1. *Producers*
Producers make their own food. Plants, like grass and trees, get their energy from the Sun.

Setting a **purpose** helps you better understand what you are reading. A purpose is a reason to do something. Your purpose for reading a textbook is to find information.

How to Set a Purpose

Ask yourself two questions before you start a new chapter. Try to answer them as you read.

What is the subject of the chapter?

What is the author saying about the subject?

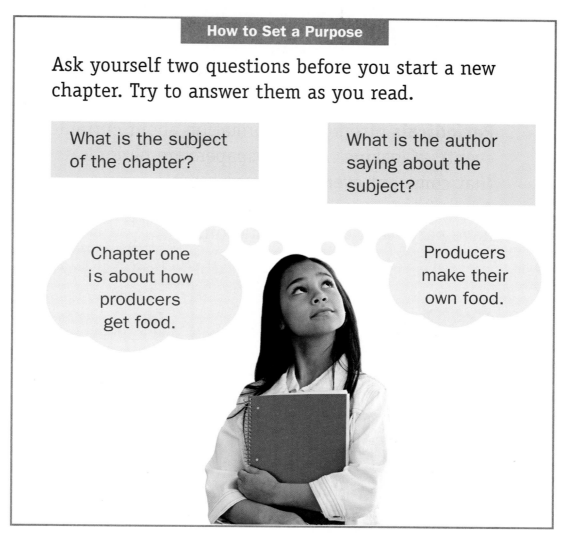

Chapter one is about how producers get food.

Producers make their own food.

WHY IT MATTERS

You read a science textbook to learn information about science topics.

Periodicals

ESSENTIAL IDEA

You read periodicals to learn new ideas and information.

Periodicals often give information about current events. Magazines and newspapers are periodicals that come out every day, week, month, or year. An **article** is a story about a topic. Articles have parts that give information.

Article Parts

headline An article's headline tells you what the article is about.

photograph Newspapers often show a picture of the topic of the article.

caption The caption gives important information about the photo.

◀ Newspapers can have many articles.

How to Preview

Preview what is in the article before you begin reading. To preview means "to look ahead."

1 Read the headline, or title, of the article.

2 Then look at any photographs in the article.

article

The Daily Tribune

headline

photograph

Students Discover New Flower

by Tamara Clark

Fourth graders made a surprising discovery on a field trip to the Florida Everglades last week. Two students spotted a bright purple orchid while walking along the trail. "It was so beautiful," said the teacher, Ms. Johansen.

"We wanted to know its scientific name."

They could not identify the flower using any classification book. That's because this colorful species of orchid had not been discovered yet.

Students want to name the new flower after their teacher.

caption

WHY IT MATTERS

Articles can give you recent information about science topics.

Internet

> **ESSENTIAL IDEA**
>
> The Internet is a fast way to search for information about science.

The Internet has lots of information. You can use a computer to **search** the Internet for facts.

First, you enter **key words** about your topic into a search engine, or a Web site that finds key words on other sites. Then you will get links to many **Web sites**.

What state of matter is snow? Is it a *solid*, *liquid*, or *gas*?

computer

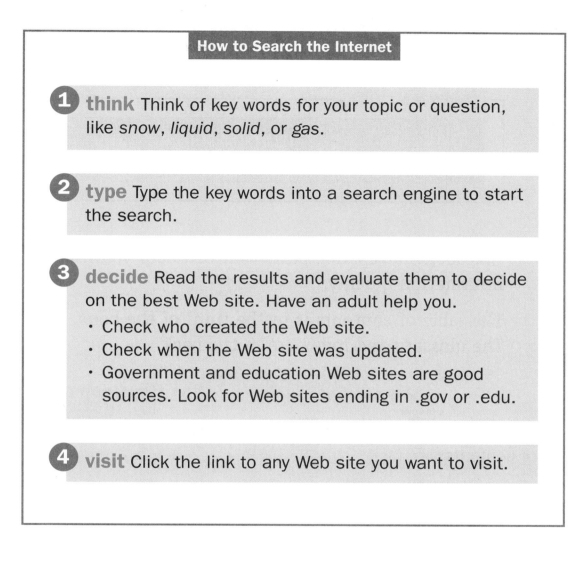

How to Search the Internet

1 think Think of key words for your topic or question, like *snow*, *liquid*, *solid*, or *gas*.

2 type Type the key words into a search engine to start the search.

3 decide Read the results and evaluate them to decide on the best Web site. Have an adult help you.
- Check who created the Web site.
- Check when the Web site was updated.
- Government and education Web sites are good sources. Look for Web sites ending in .gov or .edu.

4 visit Click the link to any Web site you want to visit.

WHY IT MATTERS

You can use the Internet to answer your questions.

You have to search the Internet using key words and then decide which sources to use.

Parts of a Textbook

ESSENTIAL IDEA

Textbooks have many parts that help you find information.

Textbooks have three parts that can help you find information quickly.

The table of contents is in the front of the book. The glossary and index are in the back.

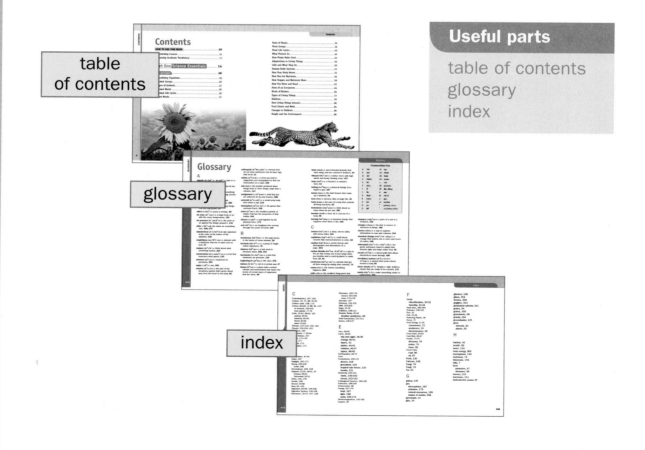

table of contents

glossary

index

Useful parts

table of contents
glossary
index

Table of Contents

The **table of contents** names the units and chapters in order. Use a table of contents to find the first page number of each unit and chapter. The table of contents page sometimes has the headline of Contents.

Contents

unit

chapter

To learn about types of animals, I should look at the chapter on page 22.

Glossary

A **glossary** lists key words used in a textbook. The glossary gives the **definition**, or meaning, of each word. A **pronunciation key** helps you say the word correctly.

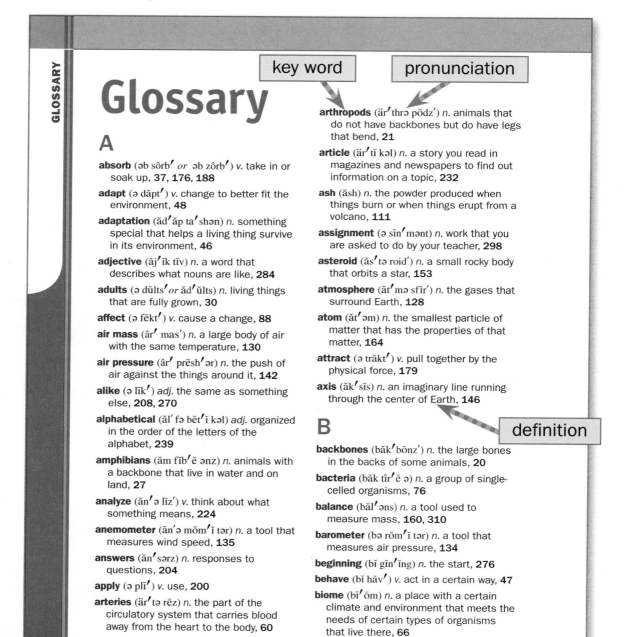

GLOSSARY

Glossary

key word   pronunciation

A

absorb (əb sôrb′ *or* əb zôrb′) *v.* take in or soak up, **37, 176, 188**

adapt (ə dăpt′) *v.* change to better fit the environment, **48**

adaptation (ăd′ăp ta′shən) *n.* something special that helps a living thing survive in its environment, **46**

adjective (ăj′ĭk tĭv) *n.* a word that describes what nouns are like, **284**

adults (ə dŭlts′ *or* ăd′ŭlts) *n.* living things that are fully grown, **30**

affect (ə fĕkt′) *v.* cause a change, **88**

air mass (âr′ mas′) *n.* a large body of air with the same temperature, **130**

air pressure (âr′ prĕsh′ər) *n.* the push of air against the things around it, **142**

alike (ə līk′) *adj.* the same as something else, **208, 270**

alphabetical (ăl′ fə bĕt′ ĭ kəl) *adj.* organized in the order of the letters of the alphabet, **239**

amphibians (ăm fĭb′ē ənz) *n.* animals with a backbone that live in water and on land, **27**

analyze (ăn′ə līz′) *v.* think about what something means, **224**

anemometer (ăn′ə mŏm′ĭ tər) *n.* a tool that measures wind speed, **135**

answers (ăn′sərz) *n.* responses to questions, **204**

apply (ə plī′) *v.* use, **200**

arteries (är′tə rēz) *n.* the part of the circulatory system that carries blood away from the heart to the body, **60**

arthropods (är′thrə pŏdz′) *n.* animals that do not have backbones but do have legs that bend, **21**

article (är′tĭ kəl) *n.* a story you read in magazines and newspapers to find out information on a topic, **232**

ash (ăsh) *n.* the powder produced when things burn or when things erupt from a volcano, **111**

assignment (ə sīn′mənt) *n.* work that you are asked to do by your teacher, **298**

asteroid (ăs′tə roid′) *n.* a small rocky body that orbits a star, **153**

atmosphere (ăt′mə sfîr′) *n.* the gases that surround Earth, **128**

atom (ăt′əm) *n.* the smallest particle of matter that has the properties of that matter, **164**

attract (ə trăkt′) *v.* pull together by the physical force, **179**

axis (ăk′sĭs) *n.* an imaginary line running through the center of Earth, **146**

definition

B

backbones (băk′bōnz′) *n.* the large bones in the backs of some animals, **20**

bacteria (băk tîr′ē ə) *n.* a group of single-celled organisms, **76**

balance (băl′əns) *n.* a tool used to measure mass, **160, 310**

barometer (bə rŏm′ĭ tər) *n.* a tool that measures air pressure, **134**

beginning (bĭ gĭn′ĭng) *n.* the start, **276**

behave (bĭ hāv′) *v.* act in a certain way, **47**

biome (bī′ōm) *n.* a place with a certain climate and environment that meets the needs of certain types of organisms that live there, **66**

Index

The **index** is a list of topics in a book. Each **entry** names a topic and lists the pages where you can read about it. Entries appear in **alphabetical** order.

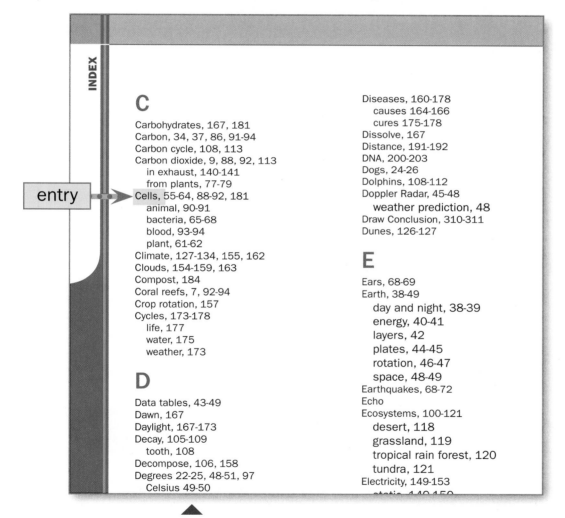

INDEX

C

Carbohydrates, 167, 181
Carbon, 34, 37, 86, 91-94
Carbon cycle, 108, 113
Carbon dioxide, 9, 88, 92, 113
   in exhaust, 140-141
   from plants, 77-79

entry → Cells, 55-64, 88-92, 181
   animal, 90-91
   bacteria, 65-68
   blood, 93-94
   plant, 61-62
Climate, 127-134, 155, 162
Clouds, 154-159, 163
Compost, 184
Coral reefs, 7, 92-94
Crop rotation, 157
Cycles, 173-178
   life, 177
   water, 175
   weather, 173

D

Data tables, 43-49
Dawn, 167
Daylight, 167-173
Decay, 105-109
   tooth, 108
Decompose, 106, 158
Degrees 22-25, 48-51, 97
   Celsius 49-50

Diseases, 160-178
   causes 164-166
   cures 175-178
Dissolve, 167
Distance, 191-192
DNA, 200-203
Dogs, 24-26
Dolphins, 108-112
Doppler Radar, 45-48
   weather prediction, 48
Draw Conclusion, 310-311
Dunes, 126-127

E

Ears, 68-69
Earth, 38-49
   day and night, 38-39
   energy, 40-41
   layers, 42
   plates, 44-45
   rotation, 46-47
   space, 48-49
Earthquakes, 68-72
Echo
Ecosystems, 100-121
   desert, 118
   grassland, 119
   tropical rain forest, 120
   tundra, 121
Electricity, 149-153
   static, 149-150

Information about cells starts on page 55.

— **WHY IT MATTERS** —

> The parts of textbooks help you find information.

239

Textbook Features

Science textbooks have different features that give you information.

Science textbooks have several **features** that give you information and help you learn.

Textbook Features

titles and headings

LIFE SCIENCE

Types of Animals

terms

Mammals

Mammals are **warm-blooded** animals. Their bodies stay at about the same temperature all the time.

All mammals breathe with **lungs**. Hair or **fur** covers all mammals. They have **limbs**.

photographs

illustrations

charts and graphs

part	roles
stem	holds up leaves and flowers
leaves	make food
roots	hold plant in soil take in water and nutrients

diagrams

animals

mammals | birds | fish | reptiles | amphibians

Titles and Headings

Titles and **headings** give clues to the main idea. You can find details about the main idea in the **graphics** you see. Graphics include tables, charts, and drawings.

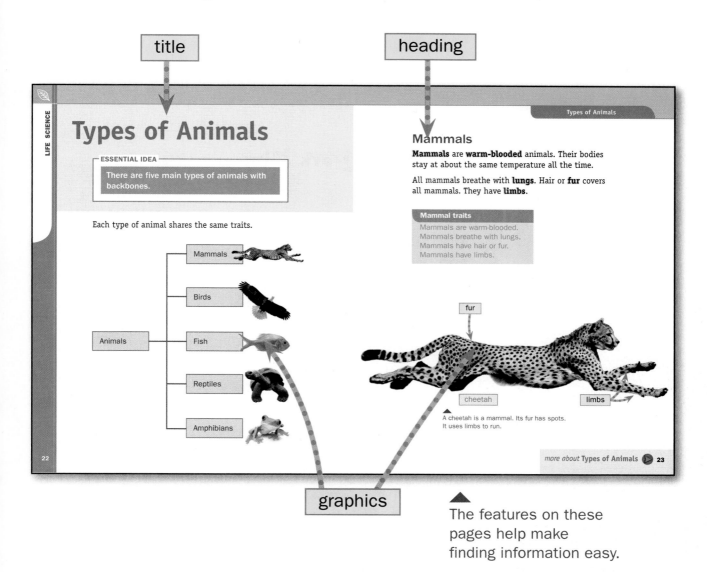

title

heading

graphics

Types of Animals

ESSENTIAL IDEA

There are five main types of animals with backbones.

Each type of animal shares the same traits.

Animals
- Mammals
- Birds
- Fish
- Reptiles
- Amphibians

Mammals

Mammals are **warm-blooded** animals. Their bodies stay at about the same temperature all the time.

All mammals breathe with **lungs**. Hair or **fur** covers all mammals. They have **limbs**.

Mammal traits
Mammals are warm-blooded.
Mammals breathe with lungs.
Mammals have hair or fur.
Mammals have limbs.

fur

cheetah

limbs

A cheetah is a mammal. Its fur has spots. It uses limbs to run.

more about Types of Animals 23

22

The features on these pages help make finding information easy.

Textbook Features *continued*

Terms to Know

Science textbooks introduce many new words. As you read, look for hints about what a new word, or **key term**, means. Often you will find a **definition** on the page.

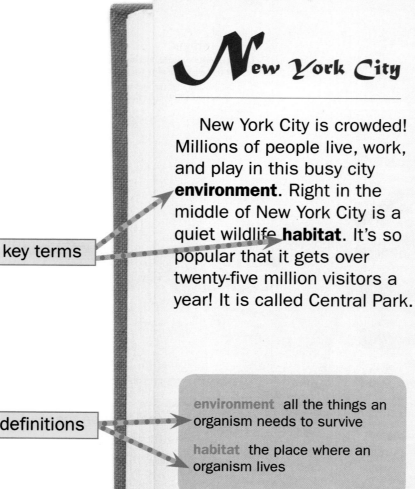

*N*ew *Y*ork *C*ity

New York City is crowded! Millions of people live, work, and play in this busy city **environment**. Right in the middle of New York City is a quiet wildlife **habitat**. It's so popular that it gets over twenty-five million visitors a year! It is called Central Park.

key terms

definitions

environment all the things an organism needs to survive

habitat the place where an organism lives

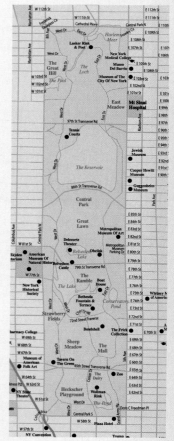

Central Park, New York City

Photographs and Illustrations

Photographs are pictures taken with a camera.
Illustrations are drawings used to explain things.
Read the **caption** near each photograph or
illustration to learn what it shows.

photograph

Central Park is surrounded by New York's skyscrapers.

caption

Charts and Graphs

Science textbooks often give details in **charts** and **graphs**. A chart **presents**, or shows, information in rows (←→) and columns (↕). A graph presents information with bars, pictures, shapes, or lines.

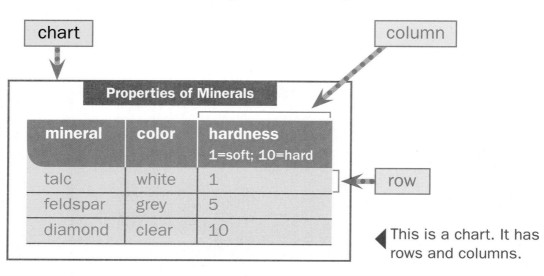

chart

column

Properties of Minerals

mineral	color	hardness 1=soft; 10=hard
talc	white	1
feldspar	grey	5
diamond	clear	10

row

◀ This is a chart. It has rows and columns.

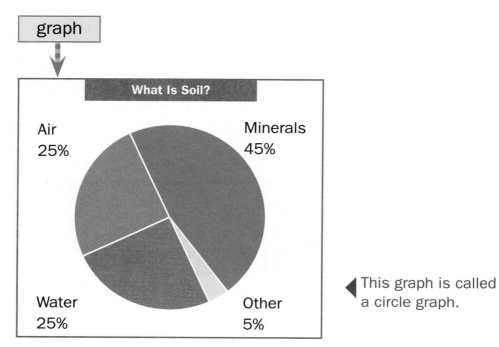

graph

What Is Soil?

Air
25%

Minerals
45%

Water
25%

Other
5%

◀ This graph is called a circle graph.

Diagrams

A **diagram** may use arrows, boxes, and words to explain something. It may **display**, or show, how parts go together or how something works.

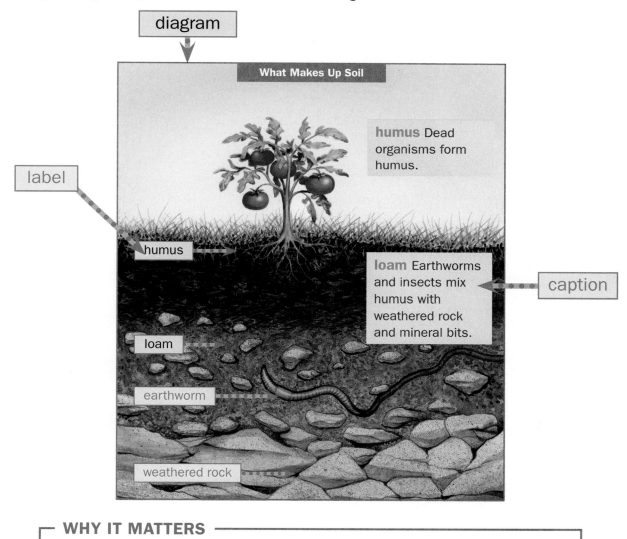

diagram

What Makes Up Soil

humus Dead organisms form humus.

label

humus

loam Earthworms and insects mix humus with weathered rock and mineral bits.

caption

loam

earthworm

weathered rock

WHY IT MATTERS

The features of a textbook help you learn in different ways.

Comprehension

Comparing and Contrasting

ESSENTIAL IDEA

Compare and contrast to figure out how things are alike and different.

You **compare** things when you look at how they are **similar**, or the same. You **contrast** things when you look at how they are **different**. Think about how the animals are similar and different in the text.

ANIMAL CHARACTERISITICS

Animals have characteristics that help them survive.

- A **camel** has four long legs and a hump. The hump doesn't hold water. The fat in the hump provides energy for the camel when food is hard to find. Camels have light brown fur.

- The **giraffe** has four long legs and a very long neck. It uses its height to reach leaves in the treetops. Shorter animals can't reach that high. Giraffes have spotted fur.

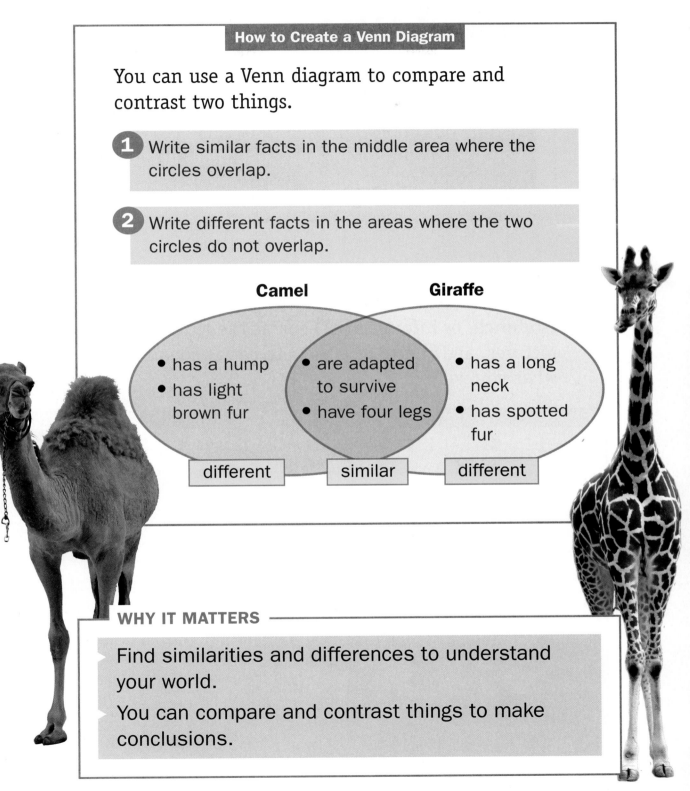

How to Create a Venn Diagram

You can use a Venn diagram to compare and contrast two things.

1 Write similar facts in the middle area where the circles overlap.

2 Write different facts in the areas where the two circles do not overlap.

Camel

Giraffe

- has a hump
- has light brown fur

- are adapted to survive
- have four legs

- has a long neck
- has spotted fur

different   similar   different

WHY IT MATTERS

Find similarities and differences to understand your world.

You can compare and contrast things to make conclusions.

Predicting

When you read, you predict by telling what you think will happen next. Use facts in the text to help you predict.

Predicting is telling what you think will happen next in the text. Before predicting, you first gather **evidence**, or information. Look at the titles, pictures, and charts on a page to get an idea about what you will read.

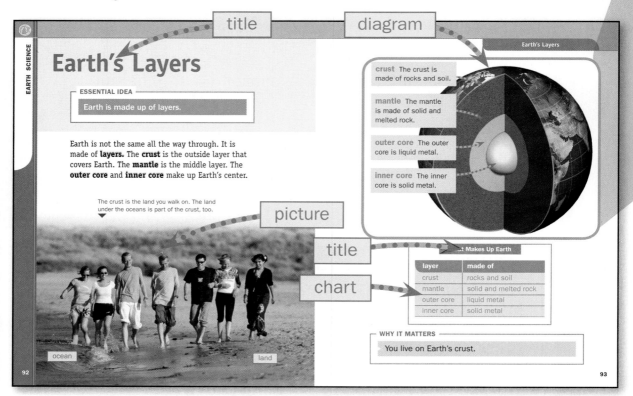

title

diagram

Earth's Layers

EARTH SCIENCE

ESSENTIAL IDEA

Earth is made up of layers.

Earth is not the same all the way through. It is made of **layers.** The **crust** is the outside layer that covers Earth. The **mantle** is the middle layer. The **outer core** and **inner core** make up Earth's center.

The crust is the land you walk on. The land under the oceans is part of the crust, too.

picture

ocean land

Earth's Layers

crust The crust is made of rocks and soil.

mantle The mantle is made of solid and melted rock.

outer core The outer core is liquid metal.

inner core The inner core is solid metal.

title

chart

...t Makes Up Earth

layer	made of
crust	rocks and soil
mantle	solid and melted rock
outer core	liquid metal
inner core	solid metal

WHY IT MATTERS

You live on Earth's crust.

92

93

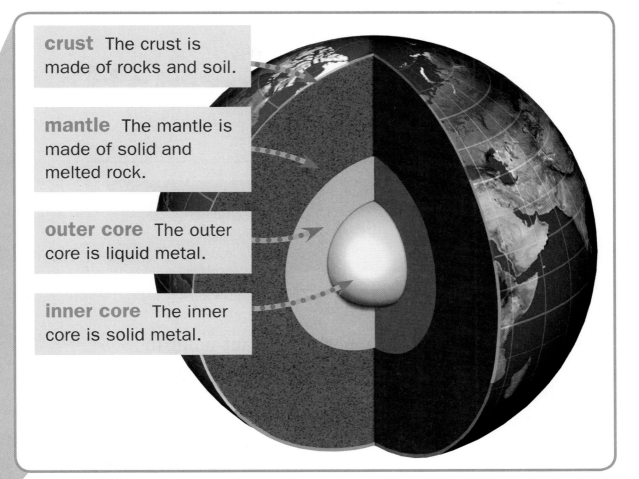

crust The crust is made of rocks and soil.

mantle The mantle is made of solid and melted rock.

outer core The outer core is liquid metal.

inner core The inner core is solid metal.

By looking at this illustration, you might predict that you will read about the different layers of Earth. You will also probably read about what is in each layer.

WHY IT MATTERS

You use pictures, charts, and titles to gather information about what you will read.

You make predictions to help you understand what you read.

Determining Important Information

Identify the main idea to understand what you read. Then look for the details about the main idea.

The **main idea** is the most important point to understand. **Details** are small facts or bits of information that **support** the main idea. Think about the main idea as you read.

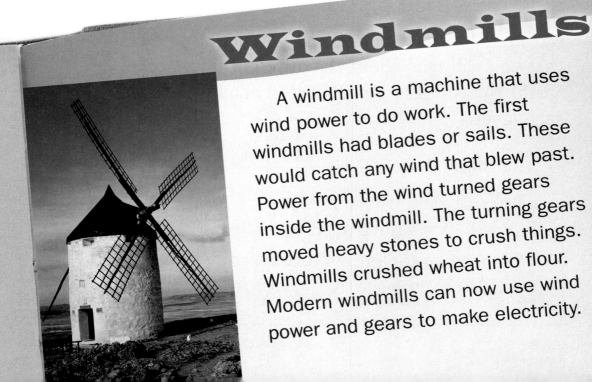

Windmills

A windmill is a machine that uses wind power to do work. The first windmills had blades or sails. These would catch any wind that blew past. Power from the wind turned gears inside the windmill. The turning gears moved heavy stones to crush things. Windmills crushed wheat into flour. Modern windmills can now use wind power and gears to make electricity.

You can make a main idea and supporting detail chart.

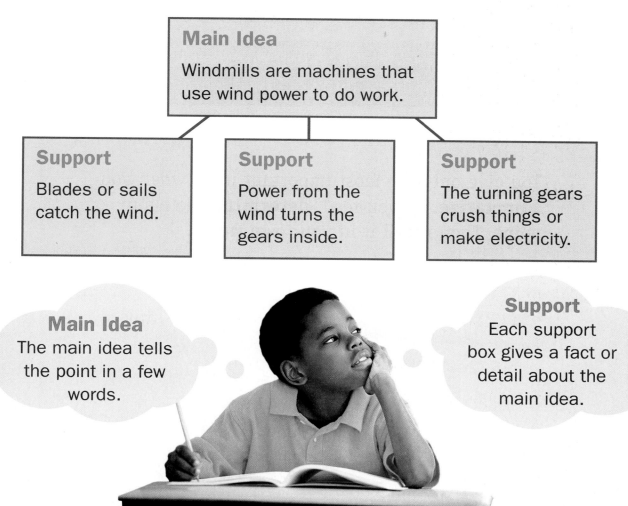

Main Idea

Windmills are machines that use wind power to do work.

Support

Blades or sails catch the wind.

Support

Power from the wind turns the gears inside.

Support

The turning gears crush things or make electricity.

Main Idea
The main idea tells the point in a few words.

Support
Each support box gives a fact or detail about the main idea.

WHY IT MATTERS

> The main idea can help you remember what is most important.

> The supporting details give you more information about the topic.

Summarizing

ESSENTIAL IDEA

You summarize when you put the most important ideas into your own words.

You give only the most important ideas when you **summarize**. As you read, **determine** the main point. Then **retell** it in your own words.

The Great Lakes Area

The Great Lakes area is always changing. Some changes happen so slowly you may not notice them. Wind blows rocks and dirt into new hills called dunes. Water carries stones and soil from place to place. Water also wears away the shoreline. Weather can cause rocks to crack or break off. Bit by bit, day by day, and year by year, the Great Lakes area is changing.

dune

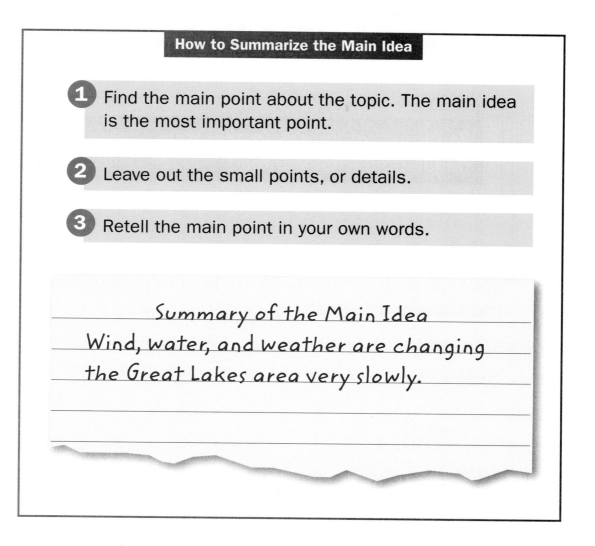

How to Summarize the Main Idea

1 Find the main point about the topic. The main idea is the most important point.

2 Leave out the small points, or details.

3 Retell the main point in your own words.

> Summary of the Main Idea
> Wind, water, and weather are changing the Great Lakes area very slowly.

WHY IT MATTERS

> You can remember what you read when you summarize ideas in your own words.

Making Inferences

ESSENTIAL IDEA

You make inferences to help you understand what you read.

Sometimes you need to connect **clues** from what you read with your own experiences to understand the meaning of a text.

This **strategy** is called making an **inference**. Use what you already know to make sense of the text.

How Energy Moves

Energy is the ability to move or change. Energy can move from one object to another. Think about playing with marbles. You roll one marble to try to hit another. The rolling marble stops when it hits the target marble. Then the target marble starts to roll. Your energy started it all!

How To Make Inferences

Making inferences is like filling in the blanks. Use your own ideas and experience to help you.

1 **Think about what you already know about the subject.**
| Marbles aren't alive. They can't move by themselves. Something must make them move.

2 **Picture the missing details.**
| The kid makes the marble roll. That's where the energy comes from. Energy goes to the other marble.

3 **Then draw a conclusion based on your own ideas.**
| There must be lots of ways for energy to move or change things.

WHY IT MATTERS

You make inferences by filling in information.

Connecting what you read to your own ideas helps you add meaning.

Visualizing

ESSENTIAL IDEA

Visualizing helps you picture what you are reading.

You **visualize** something by making a picture of it in your **mind**. Use the details given in the text to help "draw" the **image** or picture as you read.

Moons

You can see Earth's Moon in the sky. Other planets have moons, too. Mars has two moons. They are called Phobos and Deimos. They are some of the smallest moons we know about. Phobos and Deimos have odd, lumpy shapes. They look like potatoes with holes in them. Phobos is the larger moon. It has deep ruts and ridges on its dark surface. Deimos seems to be dusty, rocky, and icy.

How to Visualize

1 Think about the size, shape, and color.

2 Create a picture in your mind.

mind

- one larger, one smaller
- odd, lumpy shapes
- dusty and rocky
- ruts and ridges on dark surface

image

WHY IT MATTERS

Visualizing helps you understand and remember what you read.

Asking and Answering Questions

ESSENTIAL IDEA

Stop to ask and answer questions as you read. It's one way to make sure you understand the text.

Take time to **pause**, or stop, as you read. If something is **confusing**, or doesn't make sense, think about it. **Clarify** the text so that it makes sense to you.

Fossils

Fossils are the remains of life from long ago. The United States has many places where scientists can find fossils. One of these places is the Green River Formation. It is located in parts of Wyoming, Utah, and Colorado. This region is known for its many fish fossils. They are old but in good condition. Fossils of trout, catfish, perch, herring, and other fish have been found there.

Fish fossil, Green River, Wyoming

Answering Your Questions

You might ask and answer these questions as you read about fossils.

Why is the Green River Formation known for fish fossils?
fish live in rivers

What type of fish lived long ago?
trout, catfish, perch, and herring

WHY IT MATTERS

You can make sense of a text by asking and answering your own questions.

Ask questions about what confuses you or interests you.

Monitoring Comprehension

To **monitor** means to "check or keep track of." Good readers monitor **comprehension**, or how well they understand, as they read.

An echo is a sound you hear when sound waves bounce off a surface and come back to your ears. They can travel a long way. Echoes repeat over and over until they fade away.

Neighbors living in mountains used to call to each other to keep in touch. Their calls would echo off cliffs and rocks. Some mountain neighbors built and played long wooden horns. The horn sounds were louder than voices. The horn echoes were deep and rich.

Take time to go back and **reread** a new text if you don't understand something. That will help you **fix up** any confusing information. It also lets you adjust or change your thinking.

Ways to Monitor Comprehension

These strategies can help you check your understanding as you read.

Monitoring comprehension strategies

✓ Act out the situation.
✓ Find the main idea. State it in your own words.
✓ Visualize what you are reading about.
✓ Ask and answer questions about the text.
✓ List other questions.
✓ Connect the text to your own experiences.
✓ Retell the passage to a classmate.

WHY IT MATTERS

Understanding is the most important goal when you read.

You will become a better reader by checking your understanding as you read.

Identifying Cause-Effect

ESSENTIAL IDEA

Identifying cause and effect in science texts will help you understand why things happen.

Scientists study the causes and effects of events in nature. A **cause** is the reason something happens. The **effect** is what happens. The effect is the **result** of the cause.

Ice Cubes

When you make ice cubes from water, the water freezes, or changes to a solid. The temperature inside a freezer is cold. **As a result**, the water turns cold. The particles in the water slow down **because** it is cold. As the particles slow down, the particles attract each other. The particles become very close **due to** the attracting. **Therefore**, a solid forms.

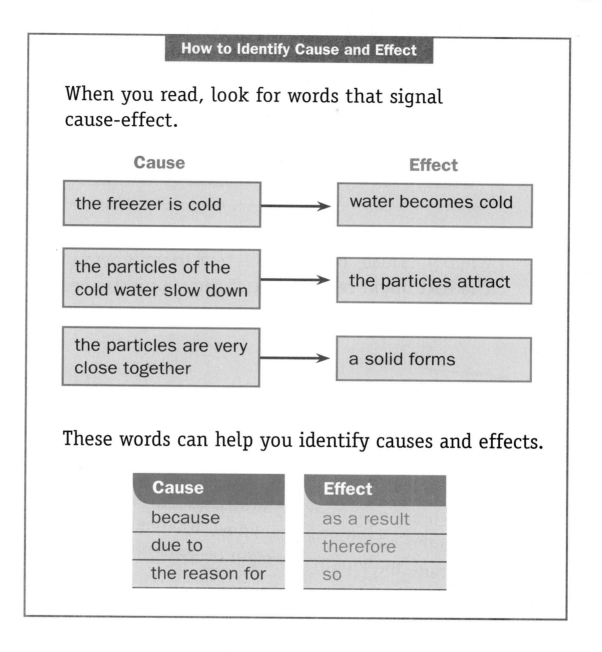

How to Identify Cause and Effect

When you read, look for words that signal cause-effect.

Cause		Effect
the freezer is cold	→	water becomes cold
the particles of the cold water slow down	→	the particles attract
the particles are very close together	→	a solid forms

These words can help you identify causes and effects.

Cause	Effect
because	as a result
due to	therefore
the reason for	so

WHY IT MATTERS

When you took a test, you may have studied (cause) and got a good grade (effect).

Making Connections

ESSENTIAL IDEA

Making connections while you read helps you to better understand the text.

When you read, **connect** the text to your own life. The text might remind you of some **experiences** that happened to you.

Science Process Skills

Estimating

Estimating is making a reasonable answer using the information you know. You might estimate the length or weight of something.

Measuring

You use tools, like a ruler, to get exact information when you measure. Units identify the numbers you measure. A centimeter and a kilometer are two common units of measurement.

Making Connections

To make connections, think about what you already know about the world. You can also make connections to other texts you have read.

1 **Think about the world.** | I know that a kilometer is more than half a mile long.

2 **Think about your own experiences.** | I estimate that my house is about three kilometers from school.

3 **Think about another text.** | I read about estimating in my math textbook.

WHY IT MATTERS

Making connections to what you read or to your experiences helps you remember the text better.

Recognizing Sequence

ESSENTIAL IDEA

Look for signal words to help you recognize the order of events.

Sequence is the **order** in which **events** take place. A process or idea will make sense to you when you can **recognize**, or see, its sequence.

Moving Water

Moving water is a powerful force. It can carve new landforms in Earth's surface. A swiftly moving river can form a new canyon. This process takes a long time. **First**, river water flows over rock. **Next**, the rock gets worn down and begins to break. **Then** the river washes away the broken rock along with sand and soil. **Finally**, a narrow valley forms.

It took millions of years for water to carve away the Grand Canyon in Arizona.

Learning words that signal sequence will help you understand the order of events in a text.

Words That Signal Sequence		
order	**sequence words**	**example**
beginning	first once in the first place at the beginning	First, water flows over rocks.
middle	next then later soon	Next, the rock wears down.
ending	finally eventually at last so	Finally, a valley forms.

WHY IT MATTERS

You use sequences when you decide what to do first, next, and last.

Generalizing

A **generalization** is an idea based on many **examples** or patterns. As you read, look for ways in which ideas are **alike**, or the same, to generalize about them.

Leaves

maple

Different plants have different kinds of leaves. Maple trees are tall and have leaves with pointy edges. Maple leaves are green in the summer and change color in the fall. You might have seen the red maple leaf on Canada's flag.

clover

Clover is a small plant with round leaves. Clover grows quickly and makes a tasty meal for cattle. Some people say that four-leaf clovers are lucky.

Cattails are tall plants that grow in marshes. Their thin leaves are very long. They can be used for weaving.

cattail

How to Make a Generalization

To make a generalization, look for examples of ideas that are alike. Decide if the ideas might be true in many cases. Then summarize the idea.

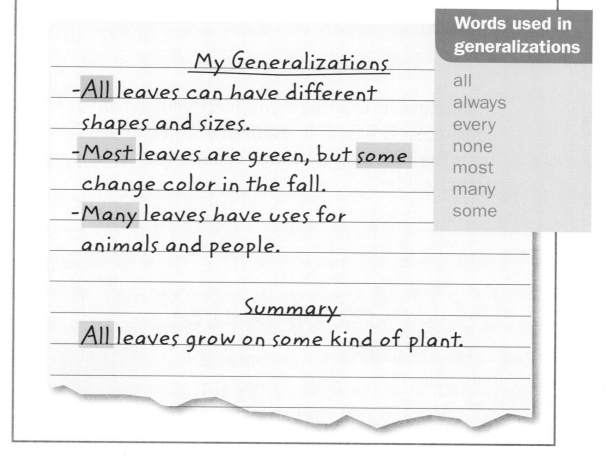

My Generalizations
-All leaves can have different shapes and sizes.
-Most leaves are green, but some change color in the fall.
-Many leaves have uses for animals and people.

Summary
All leaves grow on some kind of plant.

Words used in generalizations

all
always
every
none
most
many
some

WHY IT MATTERS

You generalize to form an idea based on facts and details.

You make generalizations when you group like things together.

Drawing a Conclusion

A **conclusion** is an idea you form yourself. A conclusion is based on **evidence**. You can use facts from the text and your own experiences to help you gather evidence.

The Color of Leaves

Trees and Leaves

Trees leaves have a chemical in them called chlorophyll. Chlorophyll is what makes leaves green. Leaves have other colors in them too, like red and yellow. The green from the chlorophyll covers up these colors. When there is not enough sunlight, the chlorophyll stops making the leaves green.

Use important facts from the text and your own experiences to help you fill in the missing information and draw a conclusion.

Drawing a Conclusion	
1 Fact	Chlorophyll uses sunlight to make tree leaves green. The green covers up the other colors in the leaves.
2 Fact	Chlorophyll stops making leaves green when there is less sunlight.
3 Experience	In lots of places, the days get shorter in the fall and winter. There is less sunlight.
4 Conclusion	Some leaves change color in the fall because they get less sunlight than in summer. The green in the leaves no longer covers the other colors.

WHY IT MATTERS

> You draw conclusions to better understand what you read.

Understanding Language

Prefixes and Suffixes

ESSENTIAL IDEA

Knowing prefixes and suffixes can help you read and understand new words.

A **prefix** is a group of letters found at the **beginning** of a word. A **suffix** is a group of letters found at the **end** of a word.

Hiking Safety

Hiking can be fun, as long as you do it safe**ly**. To avoid the possibil**ity** of dehydration, you need to plan ahead. Your survival may depend on it.

suffix →

Some places are known for their heat and dry**ness**. When the temperature gets hott**er** during the day, your body may **over**heat. When you sweat, your body **re**moves water. You need to **re**turn water back to your body. Do not make the **mis**take of running out of water. Always make sure an adult is close by.

prefix →

Learning the meanings of common prefixes and suffixes can help you figure out the meanings of new words. Read the meaning for each prefix and suffix in the chart below.

Common Prefixes and Suffixes

prefix	meaning	example
re-	again	react, recycle
over-	too much	overheat, overgrown
mis-	wrong, not	misuse, mistaken
pre-	before	prefix, preview

suffix	meaning	example
-ly	in a certain way	calmly, tightly
-er	one who, more	teacher, warmer
-ness	state or quality of	goodness
-ity	state or quality of	possibility

WHY IT MATTERS

You can understand more words when you know the meanings of prefixes and suffixes.

Cognates

Cognates are words from other languages, like **Spanish**, that mean almost the same thing in English. Cognates are spelled alike or very similarly.

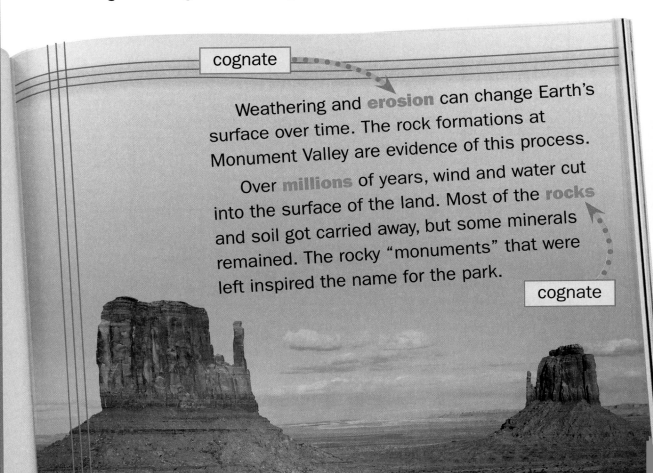

cognate

Weathering and **erosion** can change Earth's surface over time. The rock formations at Monument Valley are evidence of this process.

Over **millions** of years, wind and water cut into the surface of the land. Most of the **rocks** and soil got carried away, but some minerals remained. The rocky "monuments" that were left inspired the name for the park.

cognate

The **pronunciation** of cognates is similar. That means the word sounds the same or almost the same in both languages.

English-Spanish Cognates		
English	**Spanish**	**meaning**
conclusion	conclusión	the end
decide	decidir	to make a final choice
erosion	erosión	carrying away of Earth's surface
experiment	experimento	scientific test
hypothesis	hipótesis	prediction or guess
inferences	inferencias	conclusions based on reasoning
group	grupo	things that are together
material	material	matter, stuff
million	millón	very large number
predictions	predicciones	guesses about what will happen
process	proceso	set of steps
rocks	rocas	stones
system	sistema	group that works together

WHY IT MATTERS

> Some English words you use are shared with other languages.
> Knowing cognates can help you learn new words.

Homophones

ESSENTIAL IDEA

Homophones are words that sound alike. But they have different spellings and different meanings.

Homophones are words that have the same **sound**. They have different **spellings** and meanings.

Bees Help Flowers Grow

A **bee** is an insect that makes honey. Bees feed on nectar from flowers. Nectar is a sweet liquid. When bees get nectar from a **flower**, some yellow powder sticks **to** them. This powder is called pollen.

Pollen comes from the **male** part of a flower. When bees land on other flowers, **some** of the pollen drops onto the female parts of those flowers. This process is called pollination. Bees help plants to grow by feeding!

Say the words and choose the word that is correct for the article you just read—*be* or *bee*? *flour* or *flower*? *to, too,* or *two*? *mail* or *male*? *some* or *sum*?

Here are some other homophones that are used in science.

Homophones to Know

homophones	meanings
eye I	body part used for seeing myself
hole whole	empty place everything, all
knew new	was sure of not old
pair pear	a set of two a kind of fruit
weather whether	conditions outside if

WHY IT MATTERS

You have to be careful you don't mix up homophones when you write.

Homographs

A **homograph** is a word with one spelling but more than one meaning, or **multiple meanings**. To pick the right meaning, select the one that makes sense in the sentence. Homographs may have different **origins**.

Arizona cypress bark is made of smooth pieces that curl at the edge.

CYPRESS TREES

A cypress is a **kind** of evergreen tree. It has small, dark-green leaves that look like **scales**. Its wood is used to make doors and roofs.

Smooth-Barked Arizona Cypress trees grow in cool canyons and along streams. They have small, round cones and **bark** that looks like it's peeling. These trees grow quickly. Some can grow to be 50 feet tall. People in Arizona plant them in their **yards** to create privacy.

bark

word	meanings
bark	the sound a dog makes tough covering of a tree
kind	gentle, friendly, nice type or variety
mine	belonging to me hole dug in the earth for minerals
palm	kind of tree inside of your hand
scale	machine that weighs something a covering on the body of a fish
top	highest part a cover or lid a spinning toy
yard	unit of measure (3 feet) area surrounding a house

Some Multiple-Meaning Words

WHY IT MATTERS

You know that homographs have multiple meanings.

You need to pick the right meaning when you read a homograph in a sentence.

Comparatives and Superlatives

ESSENTIAL IDEA

Comparatives and superlatives are words used to compare two or more items.

When comparing many words, you can add an *–er* or *–est* to the end of an **adjective**. An adjective is a word that describes something. For words that cannot change, *more* or *most* is used with the word.

The Queen of the Ocean

The blue whale is the largest mammal in the animal kingdom. Blue whales grow to be about 80 feet (25 meters) long. They are also the heaviest mammals, weighing about 120 tons. The longest blue whale found was a female, which measured 94 feet long. Female whales are larger than males.

Blue whales are also the loudest animals on Earth. The blue whale's call is louder than a jet.

How to Show Comparison

Use *–er* to form the **comparative** and show **comparison** between two things. Use *–est* to form the **superlative** and show comparison between three or more things.

adjective	comparative	superlative
large	larger	largest
dark	darker	darkest
long	longer	longest
short	shorter	shortest
warm	warmer	warmest
cold	colder	coldest
light	lighter	lightest
heavy	heavier	heaviest
dry	drier	driest
wet	wetter	wettest

Some words like *dry* or *wet* change spelling before adding *–er* or *–est*.

WHY IT MATTERS

You use a comparative when you tell which of your two friends is taller.

You use a superlative when you tell which of your three friends is tallest.

Jargon

ESSENTIAL IDEA

Jargon is the language of a certain group of people.

People in some **professions** and hobbies may use words that others don't know. These words are called **jargon**. Use **context clues** to figure out the meaning of jargon.

A reporter predicts rain for areas in the low system.

Some TV news reporters talk about the weather. They use special words to predict what the weather will be. **Low**, **high**, and **front** are three words they may use. These words refer to air conditions that affect the weather. A **low** weather system usually brings clouds and rain. Look for blue skies and puffy clouds in a **high** system. A **front** is the edge between two large masses of air. Weather changes when a front passes through an area.

Low, *high*, and *front* are jargon. People who predict weather use those words because they have special meanings in their profession.

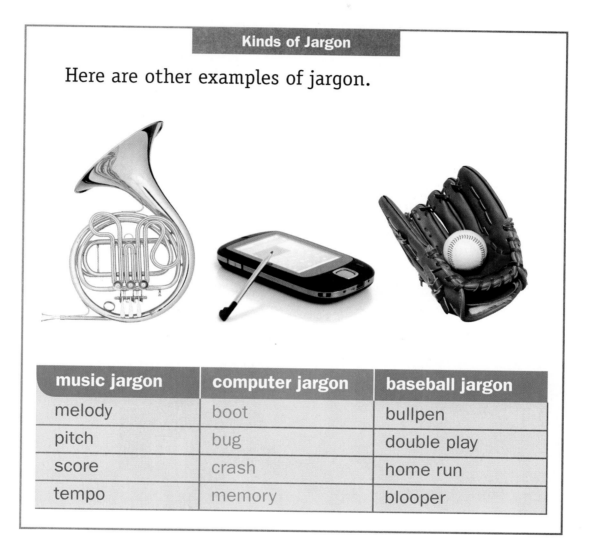

Kinds of Jargon

Here are other examples of jargon.

music jargon	computer jargon	baseball jargon
melody	boot	bullpen
pitch	bug	double play
score	crash	home run
tempo	memory	blooper

WHY IT MATTERS

You sometimes need to learn jargon to understand certain topics, like how to use a computer.

287

Understanding Idioms

ESSENTIAL IDEA

Idioms are phrases that have different meanings from the words themselves.

An **idiom** is a phrase, or group of words. The words have a different meaning when you **combine** them. For example, the idiom "it's not rocket science" means "it's not difficult to figure out."

"I thought the science test was a breeze."

more idioms for "easy"
piece of cake
a cake walk
easy as pie
no sweat

People use idioms to **express** what they are saying in an interesting way. Idioms are part of everyday conversation, or **informal language**.

Idioms to Know

Here are some common idioms you may hear.

idioms	meanings
an arm and a leg	a lot of money
down to the wire	to the very end
on pins and needles	worried about something
on the same page	agree
out of the blue	unexpectedly
pulling your leg	lying or teasing you

WHY IT MATTERS

You hear people use idioms in conversations.

You need to know idioms to understand everyday speech or writing.

Signal Words

ESSENTIAL IDEA

Signal words give clues to what you will read.

Signal words are words in sentences that give **clues** about what you are going to read. Knowing signal words helps you recognize **patterns** in what you read. The word *same* is a clue that you will be reading about a comparison.

HOME ▪ ABOUT ▪ CONTACT   🔍 [_____] SEARCH ▶

Animal Classification

Scientists divide organisms into groups or **types** that have the **same** characteristics. For example, humans and dogs are **members** of the animal kingdom. They **both** are warm-blooded and have backbones. They **belong** to the **same class**, too. Their **class** is called *mammalia*, or mammals.

Although humans and dogs share characteristics, humans and dogs are in **different** mammal groups. Scientists classify humans as *primates* in the species *sapiens*. **However**, dogs are classified as *carnivores* in the species *familiaris*.

Scientists classify organisms by how they are alike or different, or how they **relate** to one another. Signal words can help you see how things are being compared, classified, or described.

Common Signal Words in Science

comparison	classification	description
same	belong	above
different	group	under
both	type	between
however	class	over
although	members	below

WHY IT MATTERS

Recognizing signal words helps you know what you are going to read about.

You can use signal words to help organize your thoughts.

Phrasal Verbs

A **phrasal verb** is a kind of **phrase**, or a group of words that work together. A phrasal verb is a verb and one or more other words, such as *slow down*. Together the words create a meaning that is different from the **original** verb.

Understanding Force

You come across physical science daily. For example, knowing the essential idea about force can help you figure out why you travel faster on some landforms on a bicycle.

It's easy for riders to **speed up** when they **go down** a hill. The force of gravity helps them move forward. When riders **go up** a hill, they have to work harder. They **slow down** because gravity is working against them.

Learning Phrasal Verbs

Many phrasal verbs are made up of verbs and direction words, such as *up* and *down*.

phrasal verbs with "up"

stand up *with your group*
look up *the definition*
go up *to the board*
bring up *your test when finished*
speed up *your search on the computer*
sum up *the article in your own words*
write up *the report*

phrasal verbs with "down"

sit down *next to your partner*
tear down *your science exhibit*
go down *to the cafeteria*
slow down *in the hallway*
write down *your questions*
quiet down, *class is starting*
put down *the magnifying glass*

WHY IT MATTERS

You hear people use phrasal verbs every day in your classroom.

You may use phrasal verbs when you give directions.

Common Spelling Mistakes

ESSENTIAL IDEA

Some words are difficult to spell because they do not follow spelling rules. Other words are not spelled the way they sound.

Some words are easy to **misspell**. People often misspell *height* because it breaks a common spelling **rule**: Put *i* before *e*, except after *c*, or when sounded like *a* as in *neighbor* and *weigh*.

Some words have letters that are silent. You don't **pronounce**, or say, all the letters in *answer, half, high,* and *sign*.

Common Spelling Mistakes

words people misspell

receive	answer
science	half
column	high
weather	sigh

words that break the "i before e" rule

foreign	their
height	either
weird	neither

words with silent letters

answer	believe
write	guide
people	island

WHY IT MATTERS

Some words are difficult to spell because they don't follow spelling rules.

You don't pronounce the silent letters found in words like *half* and *science*.

Writing for Science

Choosing a Topic

ESSENTIAL IDEA

When you write a report for science, you need to brainstorm and choose a topic.

The first step in writing a **report** is to read the directions of your **assignment**.

Write a report that answers the question:

What is the most important invention in the past 100 years? Why? Explain your answer.

assignment

Now you know the subject of your report. Next, you need to select a **topic**, or what you are going to write about. Choose a topic for the assignment.

skateboard

Brainstorming

Brainstorming is a good way to begin. When you **brainstorm**, you think of as many ideas as you can. Collect all of your ideas in one place.

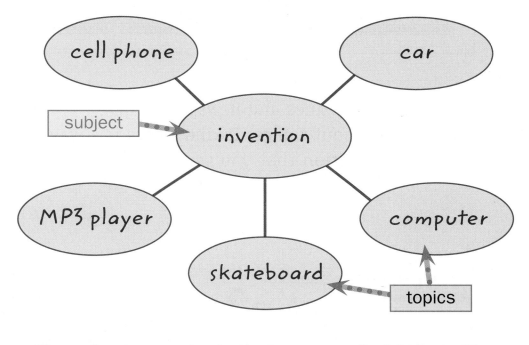

Then choose one topic that you can find information for and that interests you.

WHY IT MATTERS

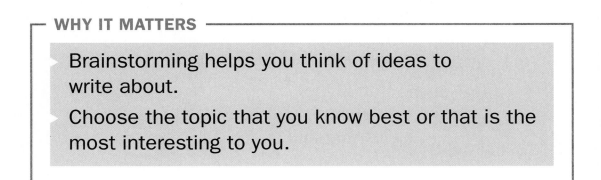

Brainstorming helps you think of ideas to write about.

Choose the topic that you know best or that is the most interesting to you.

Taking Notes

ESSENTIAL IDEA

Taking notes is a way to record important information about a topic.

Articles in magazines and newspapers give information about topics. Taking **notes** is a way to **gather** information that you want to remember.

What's an Earthquake?

Earthquakes release stress in Earth. Deep inside the crust, large blocks of Earth, called plates, collide. The plates move against each other. Stress builds up and a crack forms in the crust. The stress moves through Earth as waves. The waves are what we feel during an earthquake.

crack

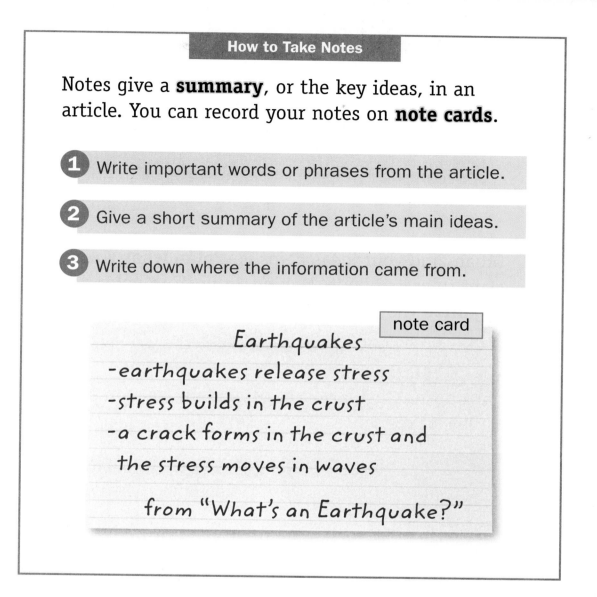

How to Take Notes

Notes give a **summary**, or the key ideas, in an article. You can record your notes on **note cards**.

1 Write important words or phrases from the article.

2 Give a short summary of the article's main ideas.

3 Write down where the information came from.

note card

Earthquakes
-earthquakes release stress
-stress builds in the crust
-a crack forms in the crust and
 the stress moves in waves

from "What's an Earthquake?"

WHY IT MATTERS

By taking notes, you record information that you can use when you write.

Organizing Ideas

ESSENTIAL IDEA

Before you begin writing, it helps to organize your information in an outline.

Organizing your ideas helps you **plan** what you want to write about. Making an **outline** helps you **organize** the information about your topic.

How to Write an Outline

An outline helps you put the main ideas in an order that makes sense.

1. First, write your topic at the top of the page.

2. Next, use Roman numerals (I, II, and III) for each main idea you want to include.

3. Then, use capital letters for each supporting idea.

4. Finally, reread your outline to make sure it makes sense.

You can create an outline based on what you know or what you read.

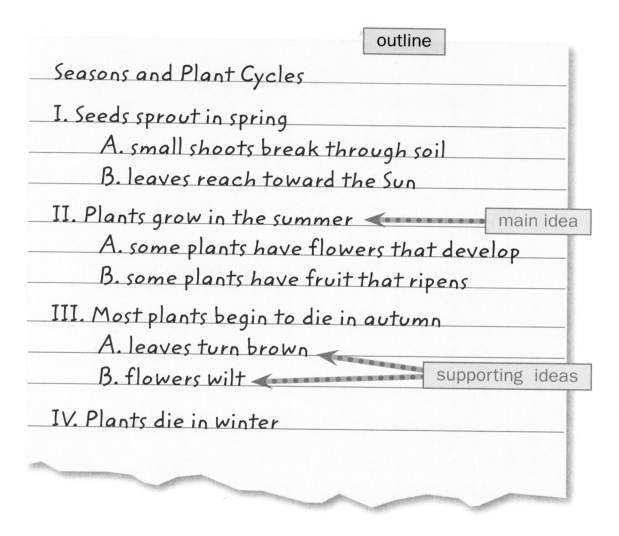

outline

Seasons and Plant Cycles

I. Seeds sprout in spring
    A. small shoots break through soil
    B. leaves reach toward the Sun

II. Plants grow in the summer   main idea
    A. some plants have flowers that develop
    B. some plants have fruit that ripens

III. Most plants begin to die in autumn
    A. leaves turn brown
    B. flowers wilt   supporting ideas

IV. Plants die in winter

WHY IT MATTERS

Making an outline helps you organize your ideas before you begin to write.

Drafting and Revising

ESSENTIAL IDEA

Use an outline to write a draft. Then revise the draft to make it better.

First, use the ideas from your outline to create a **draft**. Then you can **revise** it, or rewrite it to make it better.

Ask questions to help you **improve** your revision. Make sure all of your words are clear and **precise**.

draft

> People from Egypt used levers to make pyramids. The rock was too heavy to lift. They put a log on a pointy stone. Then they used levers to lift the heavy rock. They put a heavy weight on the other side. This raised the log and pushed the rock up.

How to Revise

1 **Add details.**	I added the detail, *In ancient times.*
2 **Use precise words.**	The words *Egyptians* and *fulcrum* are precise.
3 **Make sure sentences are clear.**	I rewrote some of my sentences.

revision

In ancient times, Egyptians used levers to build pyramids. To lift a heavy rock, they placed a log on a pointed stone, called a fulcrum. Then they put one side of the log under the heavy rock. On the opposite side, they laid a weight. The heavy weight raised the rock they used for the pyramid.

WHY IT MATTERS

Revising is an important step in improving your writing.

Editing and Proofreading

ESSENTIAL IDEA

Editing and proofreading are ways to make your writing clear and correct.

After you are done revising, reread your paper one last time. When you **edit**, you read it again to make sure the sentences are clear and **flow** together.

Proofread your writing to make sure that all words are spelled correctly. Then make sure each sentence has the correct **punctuation**.

If you want to help save the environment, remember to ~~reduse~~ reduce, reuse, and recycle. You can reduce trash by using fewer resources. For example, you can carry a cloth shopping bag instead of using a plastic one. You can also reuse things instead of throwing them out. A shoebox can be used for storing things rather ~~then~~ than having them end up in a landfill. Recycling is important, ~~to~~ too. When you recycle paper and cans, they can be made into ~~knew~~ new products.

How to Edit and Proofread Your Work

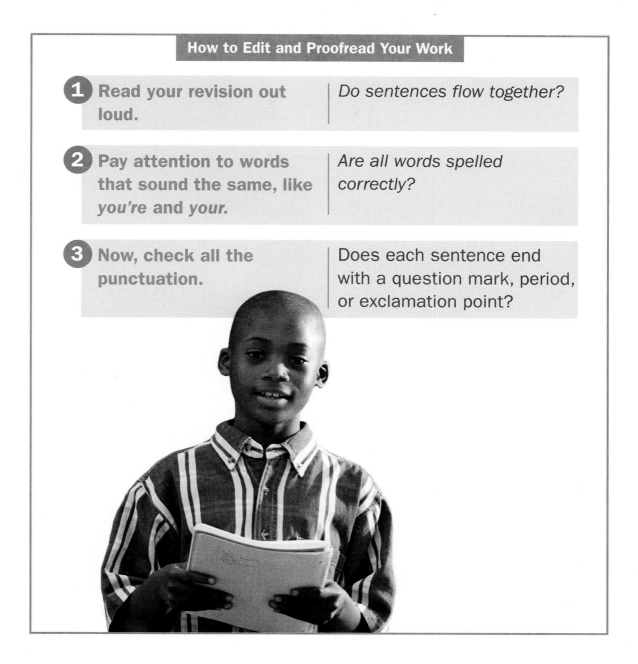

1 Read your revision out loud. | *Do sentences flow together?*

2 Pay attention to words that sound the same, like *you're* and *your*. | *Are all words spelled correctly?*

3 Now, check all the punctuation. | Does each sentence end with a question mark, period, or exclamation point?

WHY IT MATTERS

Editing and proofreading will make your writing the best it can be.

Science References

Science Tools

ESSENTIAL IDEA

Science tools help you make observations.

Some science tools help you measure and compare things.

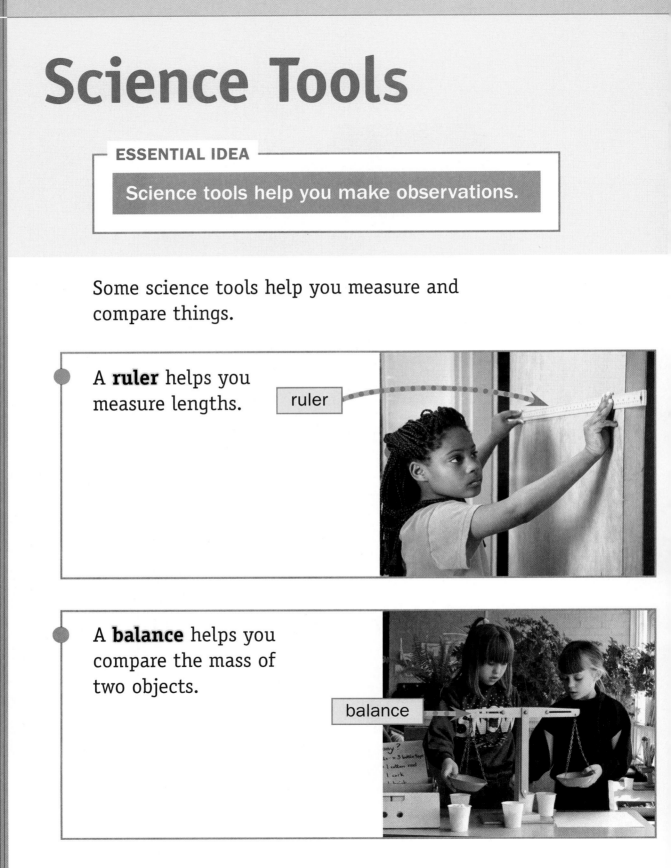

- A **ruler** helps you measure lengths.

  ruler

- A **balance** helps you compare the mass of two objects.

  balance

A **graduated cylinder** can help you measure the volume, or amount, of a liquid.

graduated cylinder

A **magnifying lens** makes objects look bigger so you can see more details.

magnifying lens

WHY IT MATTERS

You use science tools to explore the world around you.

Standard and Metric Units

ESSENTIAL IDEA

Two systems are used for measuring.

In the United States, most people use the **standard system** for measuring. Scientists, however, use the **metric system** all over the world.

metric system

A ruler measures length.

standard system

Length and Distance Conversions

metric units

1 centimeter (cm)	=	10 millimeters (mm)
1 decimeter (dm)	=	10 centimeters (cm)
1 meter (m)	=	100 centimeters (cm)
1 kilometer (km)	=	1,000 meters (m)

standard units

1 foot (ft)	=	12 inches (in.)
1 yard (yd)	=	3 feet (ft)
1 mile (mi)	=	5,280 feet (ft)

Mass and Weight Conversions

metric units

1 gram (g)	= 1,000 milligrams (mg)
1 kilogram (kg)	= 1,000 grams (g)

standard units

1 pound (lb)	= 16 ounces (oz)
1 ton (t)	= 2,000 pounds (lb)

This balance measures the apple's mass.

Volume Conversions

metric units

1 liter (L)	= 1,000 milliliters (mL)

standard units

1 pint (pt)	= 2 cups (c)
1 quart (qt)	= 2 pints (pt)
1 gallon (gal)	= 8 pints (pt)

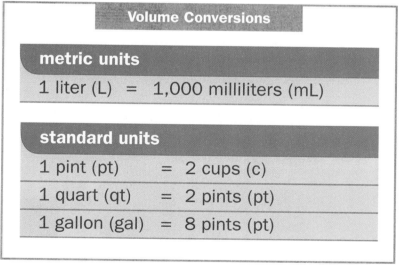

A measuring cup measures volume.

WHY IT MATTERS

You can use two systems of measurement in science class and in your life.

313

Science Safety

ESSENTIAL IDEA

Follow the rules to be safe when doing science experiments.

Be careful when you do a science experiment, and you will not get hurt. Always wear **goggles** when you do an experiment.

goggles

▲

Goggles can protect your eyes when you do experiments.

Safety Rules

1 Read all the directions before you start.

2 Clean your work area before and after an experiment. Clean up spills immediately.

3 Make sure your teacher is around when working with thermometers and other materials.

4 Do not taste or smell anything, unless told to do so by your teacher.

5 Wash your hands when you are done.

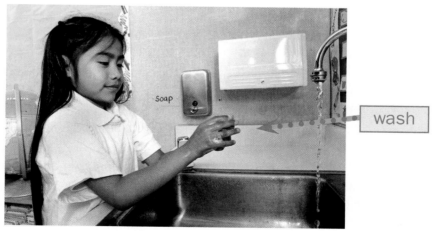

Soap   wash

WHY IT MATTERS

You can keep safe when doing science experiments by following the rules.

Glossary

A

absorb (əb sôrb′ *or* əb zôrb′) *v.* take in or soak up, **37, 176, 188**

adapt (ə dăpt′) *v.* change to better fit the environment, **48**

adaptation (ăd′ăp ta′shən) *n.* something special that helps a living thing survive in its environment, **46**

adjective (ăj′ĭk tĭv) *n.* a word that describes what nouns are like, **284**

adults (ə dŭlts′ *or* ăd′ŭlts) *n.* living things that are fully grown, **30**

affect (ə fĕkt′) *v.* cause a change, **88**

air mass (âr′ mas′) *n.* a large body of air with the same temperature, **130**

air pressure (âr′ prĕsh′ər) *n.* the push of air against the things around it, **142**

alike (ə līk′) *adj.* the same as something else, **208, 270**

alphabetical (ăl′ fə bĕt′ĭ kəl) *adj.* organized in the order of the letters of the alphabet, **239**

amphibians (ăm fĭb′ē ənz) *n.* animals with a backbone that live in water and on land, **27**

analyze (ăn′ə līz′) *v.* think about what something means, **224**

anemometer (ăn′ə mŏm′ĭ tər) *n.* a tool that measures wind speed, **135**

answers (ăn′sərz) *n.* responses to questions, **204**

apply (ə plī′) *v.* use, **200**

arteries (är′tə rēz) *n.* the part of the circulatory system that carries blood away from the heart to the body, **60**

arthropods (är′thrə pŏdz′) *n.* animals that do not have backbones but do have legs that bend, **21**

article (är′tĭ kəl) *n.* a story you read in magazines and newspapers to find out information on a topic, **232**

ash (ăsh) *n.* the powder produced when things burn or when things erupt from a volcano, **111**

assignment (ə sīn′mənt) *n.* work that you are asked to do by your teacher, **298**

asteroid (ăs′tə roid′) *n.* a small rocky body that orbits a star, **153**

atmosphere (ăt′mə sfîr′) *n.* the gases that surround Earth, **128**

atom (ăt′əm) *n.* the smallest particle of matter that has the properties of that matter, **164**

attract (ə trăkt′) *v.* pull together by the physical force, **179**

axis (ăk′sĭs) *n.* an imaginary line running through the center of Earth, **146**

B

backbones (băk′bōnz′) *n.* the large bones in the backs of some animals, **20**

bacteria (băk tîr′ē ə) *n.* a group of single-celled organisms, **76**

balance (băl′əns) *n.* a tool used to measure mass, **160, 310**

barometer (bə rŏm′ĭ tər) *n.* a tool that measures air pressure, **134**

beginning (bĭ gĭn′ĭng) *n.* the start, **276**

behave (bĭ hāv′) *v.* act in a certain way, **47**

biome (bī′ōm) *n.* a place with a certain climate and environment that meets the needs of certain types of organisms that live there, **66**

birds (bûrdz) *n.* warm-blooded animals that have wings and are covered in feathers, **24**

blizzard (blĭz′ərd) *n.* a winter storm with high winds and heavy, blowing snow, **143**

body (bŏd′ē) *n.* a human's or animal's form, **53**

boiling (boi′lĭng) *n.* a physical change from liquid to gas, **166**

bones (bōnz) *n.* the hard tissues that make up a skeleton, **54**

born (bôrn) *v.* become alive or begin life, **30**

brain (brān) *n.* the part of a body that controls all living functions, **63**

brainstorm (brān′stôrm′) *v.* think about as many ideas as you can, **299**

breathe (brēth) *v.* force air in and out of a body, **58**

burning (bûr′nĭng) *n.* a chemical change that happens when there is fire, **168**

C

canyon (kăn′yən) *n.* a deep, narrow valley with steep sides, **104**

capillaries (kăp′ə lĕr′ēz) *n.* small blood vessels that connect arteries to veins, **58**

caption (kăp′shən) *n.* words that go with photographs and illustrations on a page, **243**

carbon dioxide (kär′bən dī ŏk′sīd′) *n.* a gas in the air that comes out of your lungs when you breathe and is used by plants to make food, **32, 45**

carnivores (kär′nə vôrz′) *n.* animals that get all their energy by eating other animals, **74**

cause (kôz) *n.* the reason something happens, **264**

cells (sĕlz) *n.* the smallest living parts that make up all living things, **50, 52**

Pronunciation Key

ă	bat	oi	toy
ā	ape	ou	shout
âr	**air**	o͝o	book
ä	father	o͞o	moon
ĕ	let	s	sun
ē	ea**s**y	sh	pre**ss**ure
ĭ	if	th	**the, thing**
ī	lie	ŭ	nut
îr	**dear**	ûr	circle
k	**c**ause	ə	ago
ŏ	lot	ər	moth**er**
ō	go	′	primary stress
ô	all	‚	secondary stress

chapters (chăp′tərz) *n.* parts of a unit in a textbook, **230**

charges (chärjz) *n.* the lack or excess of electrons in things, **180**

charts (chärts) *n.* a way to organize information in rows and columns, **244**

chemical change (kĕm′ĭ kəl chānj) *n.* a change that makes one or more new forms of matter, **168**

chlorophyll (klôr′ə fĭl *or* klōr′ə fĭl) *n.* the green substance found in plants that absorbs light and helps make food, **45**

circuit (sûr′kĭt) *n.* a closed path that allows electricity to move through, **180**

circulatory system (sûr′kyə lə tôr ē sĭs′təm) *n.* a system that moves blood around a body, **60**

cirrus clouds (sîr′əs kloudz) *n.* high, feathery clouds that are made of ice crystals, **133**

clarify (klăr′ə fī) *v.* make something easier to understand, **260**

classify (klăs′ə fī′) *v.* put things into groups, **208**

climate (klī′mĭt) *n.* the usual weather of a place, **66**

clouds (kloudz) *n.* a group of water drops or ice crystals that float in the sky, **132**

clues (klo͞oz) *n.* facts that help you solve a problem, **256**, **290**

cognates (kŏg′nāts) *n.* words from different languages that have almost the same meanings and spellings, **278**

cold-blooded (kōld′blŭd′ĭd) *adj.* having a body temperature that changes when the surroundings change, **26**

collecting data (kŏ lĕkt′ĭng dā′tə *or* kŏ lĕkt′ĭng dăt′ə) *v.* making observations and measurements, **222**

collection (kə lĕk′shən) *n.* the last stage in the water cycle where water comes together in the soil as groundwater, **126**

colors (kŭl′ərz) *n.* sensations you see as light reflects off things; examples are blue and red, **188**

combine (kəm bīn′) *v.* put together, **45**, **288**

comet (kŏm′ĭt) *n.* a chunk of ice and dust that orbits the Sun, **153**

communicate (kə myo͞o′nĭ kāt′) *v.* share information with other people, **216**

community (kə myo͞o′nĭ tē) *n.* populations of different organisms in an ecosystem, **65**

comparative (kəm păr′ə tĭv) *n.* an adjective used to compare two things, **285**

compare (kəm pâr′) *v.* look for ways that things are the same, **248**

comparison (kəm pâr′ĭ sən) *n.* the way that two or more things are alike, **285**

compass (kŭm′pəs *or* kŏm′pəs) *n.* a tool that uses a magnet to show you direction, **183**

compete (kəm pēt′) *v.* fight against one another, **81**

comprehension (kŏm′prĭ hĕn′shən) *n.* understanding of a topic, **262**

computers (kəm pyo͞o′tərz) *n.* tools that compute or make information ready to use, **200**

conclusion (kən klo͞o′shən) *n.* a decision based on what you know or have read, **224**, **272**

condensation (kŏn′dĕn sā′shən *or* kŏn′dən sa′shən) *n.* when water vapor changes into water to form clouds, **127**

condense (kən dĕns′) *v.* cause a gas to change into a liquid, **127**

conduction (kən dŭk′shən) *n.* what happens when heat energy moves from one substance to another, **174**

conductors (kən dŭk′tərz) *n.* substances that allow energy to move through it easily, **174**, **180**

cones (kōnz) *n.* the round or long bunches of wood scales that hold the seeds of a plant, usually a tree, **38**

confusing (kən fyo͞oz′ĭng) *adj.* doesn't make sense, **260**

conifers (kŏn′ə fərz *or* kō′nə fərz) *n.* plants that grow their seeds inside cones, **38**

connect (kə nĕkt′) *v.* bring things together; think about how something reminds you of another thing, **266**

conserve (kən sûrv′) *v.* save or not use, **123**

consumers (kən so͞o′mərz) *n.* living things that must eat other living things to get their energy, **73**

context clues (kŏn′tĕkst′ klo͞oz) *n.* information that you use to understand a word or words you don't know, **286**

contrast (kən trăst′ *or* kŏn′trăst′) *v.* look for ways that things are different, **248**

convection (kən vĕk′shən) *n.* what happens when liquids and gases carry heat energy with them when they move, **175**

crust (krŭst) *n.* the outside layer that covers Earth, **92**

cumulonimbus clouds (kyōōm′ yə lō nĭm′bəs kloudz′) *n.* big, dark, rain clouds that grow up and down, **133**

cumulus clouds (kyōōm′ yə ləs kloudz′) *n.* puffy, white clouds with flat bases, **133**

current (kûr′ənt *or* kŭr′ənt) *n.* the flow of electric charges through a circuit, **180**

cycle (sī′kəl) *n.* a set of events where the last event leads back to the first event, **40**

cytoplasm (sī′tə plăz′əm) *n.* a clear substance, like jelly, that goes around the nucleus of a cell, **50**

D

damage (dăm′ĭj) *n.* harm, **140**

data (dā′tə *or* dăt′ə) *n.* information, **222**

decay (dĭ kā′) *v.* break apart; rot, **116**

decomposers (dē′ kəm pō′zərz) *n.* living things that feed on dead plants and animals, **76**

definition (dĕf′ə nĭsh′ən) *n.* the meaning of a word, **238, 242**

density (dĕn′sĭ tē) *n.* the amount of mass of a certain volume of matter, **162**

depend (dĭ pĕnd) *v.* need for survival, **78**

deposition (dĕp′ə zĭsh′ən) *n.* what happens when wind and water put down loose rocks and sediment, **107**

deserts (dĕz′ərts) *n.* dry biomes that get little rain and have few plants, **68**

Glossary

Pronunciation Key

ă	bat	oi	toy
ā	ape	ou	shout
âr	**air**	ŏŏ	book
ä	father	ōō	moon
ĕ	let	s	sun
ē	**ea**sy	sh	pressure
ĭ	if	th	**the, thing**
ī	lie	ŭ	nut
îr	dear	ûr	circle
k	cause	ə	ago
ŏ	lot	ər	mother
ō	go	′	primary stress
ô	all	′	secondary stress

details (dĭ tālz′ *or* dē′tālz′) *n.* small facts or pieces of information that support the main idea, **252**

determine (dĭ tûr′mĭn) *v.* decide or find, **254**

diagram (dī′ə grăm′) *n.* a picture that may use arrows, boxes, and words to describe something, **216, 245**

different (dĭf′ər ənt *or* dĭf′rənt) *adj.* not the same as something else, **208, 248**

digest (dī jĕst′ *or* dĭ jĕst′) *v.* break down food, **57**

digestive system (dī jĕs′tĭv sĭs′təm *or* dĭ jĕs′tĭv sĭs′təm) *n.* the group of parts that work together to break down food, **56**

direction (dĭ rĕk′shən *or* dī rĕk′shən) *n.* the path that something moves in, **192**

display (dĭ splā′) *v.* show, **245**

dissolve (dĭ zŏlv′) *v.* become part of a liquid, **167**

distance (dĭs′təns) *n.* the space between two objects or places, **191**

draft (drăft) *n.* written ideas in an unfinished form for a report, **304**

dry (drī) *adj.* not wet, **68**

E

earthquake (ûrth′kwāk′) *n.* a sudden movement in Earth's crust, **114**

echo (ĕk′ō) *n.* a sound that has bounced off a hard surface and comes back to your ears, **185**

ecosystem (ĕk′ō sĭs′təm *or* ē′kō sĭs′təm) *n.* all the nonliving and living things in a given area, **64**

edit (ĕd′ĭt) *v.* read something to make sure the sentences are clear and flow together, **306**

effect (ĭ fĕkt′) *n.* the result or outcome of events, **264**

electricity (ĭ lĕk trĭs′ĭ tē *or* e′lĕk trĭs′ĭ tē) *n.* a form of energy that involves the flow of electrical charges, **180**

element (ĕl′ə mənt) *n.* a substance made up of only one kind of matter, **164**

end (ĕnd) *n.* the last part, **276**

endanger (ĕn dān′jər) *v.* put a living thing in danger of not surviving, **86**

energy (ĕn′ər jē) *n.* what is needed to make things move or do work, **28, 119, 170**

entry (ĕn′trē) *n.* something on a list, **239**

environment (ĕn vī′rən mənt *or* ĕn vī′ərn mənt) *n.* the living and nonliving things that surround organisms, **28, 48, 88**

epicenter (ĕp′ĭ sĕn′tər) *n.* a point on Earth's surface above the focus of an earthquake, **115**

equator (ĭ kwā′tər) *n.* an imaginary line that divides Earth halfway between the north pole and south pole, **148**

erode (ĭ rōd′) *v.* wear away, **98, 107**

erosion (ĭ rō′zhən) *n.* what happens when wind and water carry loose rocks and sediment away, **107**

erupt (ĭ rŭpt′) *v.* burst open very quickly, **110**

esophagus (ĭ sŏf′ə gəs) *n.* a long tube that forces food into the stomach, **56**

estimate (ĕs′tə māt′) *v.* form a reasonable answer based on what you know, **210**

evaporation (ĭ văp′ə rā′shən) *n.* what happens when something changes from a liquid to a gas, **127**

events (ĭ vĕnts′) *n.* things that happen, **268**

evidence (ev′ĭ dəns) *n.* information used to decide if something is true or not, **100, 250, 272**

exact (ĭg zăkt) *adj.* carefully measured, **211**

examples (ĭk zăm′pəlz) *n.* things that can help you understand ideas, **270**

exosphere (ĕk′sō sfîr) *n.* the layer of the atmosphere that is farthest away from Earth's surface, **128**

expand (ĭk spănd′) *v.* become bigger, **106**

experiences (ĭk spîr′ē əns əs) *n.* events that happened to you, **266**

experiment (ĭk spĕr′ə mənt) *n.* a scientific test, **220**

express (ĭk sprĕs′) *v.* tell; make something known, **289**

extinct (ĭk stĭngkt′) *adj.* no longer found in nature, **87**

F

fault (fôlt) *n.* the place where two plates move past each other, **113**

feathers (fĕth′ərz) *n.* the soft things that cover the bodies of birds, **24**

features (fē′chərz) *n.* special qualities or characteristics about something, **240**

fins (fĭns) *n.* the parts of a fish that help it swim, **25**

fish (fĭsh) *n.* cold-blooded animals that have gills, scales, a backbone, and live in water, **25**

fix up (fĭks ŭp) *v.* make better, **263**

flow (flō) *n.* movement that is not broken, **180;** *v.* move along smoothly, **306**

flowering plants (flou′ər ĭng plănts) *n.* plants that grow their seeds inside flowers, **38**

flowers (flou′ərz) *n.* the parts of some plants that make seeds, **38**

focus (fo′kəs) *n.* the place where rock first breaks apart in an earthquake, **115**

food chain (fōod′ chān) *n.* something that shows what organisms eat in a habitat, **84**

food web (fōod′ wĕb) *n.* a group of many food chains for one habitat, **85**

force (fôrs *or* fōrs) *n.* what causes something to change, move, or do work, **192, 194**

forecast (fôr′kăst) *n.* a prediction about the weather, **136**

forests (fôr′ĭsts *or* fŏr′ĭsts) *n.* biomes that have many trees, **70**

fossil fuels (fŏs′əl fyōo′əlz) *n.* natural, non-renewable resources that come from the remains of old plants and animals, **121**

fossils (fŏs′elz) *n.* evidence of the remains of organisms that lived and died long ago, **100**

Glossary

Pronunciation Key

ă	bat	oi	toy
ā	ape	ou	shout
âr	**air**	ŏŏ	book
ä	father	ōō	moon
ĕ	let	s	sun
ē	easy	sh	pressure
ĭ	if	th	**the, thing**
ī	lie	ŭ	nut
îr	**dear**	ûr	circle
k	**cause**	ə	ago
ŏ	lot	ər	mother
ō	go	′	primary stress
ô	all	′	secondary stress

freezing (frēz′ĭng) *v.* change from a liquid to a solid, **166**

freshwater (frĕsh′wô tər *or* frĕsh′wŏt ər) *n.* water that you can use; about three percent of Earth's water, **125**

friction (frĭk′shən) *n.* a force that happens when two things rub against each other, **193**

front (frŭnt) *n.* the area where two air masses meet, **130**

fulcrum (fōol′krəm *or* fŭl′krəm) *n.* a fixed point, **198**

fungi (fŭn′jī *or* fŭng′gī) *n.* decomposers that feed on dead plants and animals, **76**

fur (fûr) *n.* thick hair that covers the body of a mammal, **23**

G

galaxy (găl′ək sē) *n.* a huge collection of stars, gas, and dust, **145**

gas (găs) *n.* the state of matter that will fill whatever it is put in; the particles in a gas are more spread out than the particles in both solids and liquids, **158**

gather (găth′ər) *n.* bring together in one place, **300**

generalization (jĕn′ ər ə lĭ zā′ shən) *n.* a broad idea based on many examples or patterns, **270**

germinate (jûr′mə nāt) *v.* cause or start to grow, **41**

gills (gĭlz) *n.* things that help fish breathe underwater, **25**

glacier (glā′shər) *n.* a slow-moving mass of ice and snow, **108**

glossary (glô′sə rē *or* glŏs′ə rē) *n.* the part of a book that lists key words and their definitions, **238**

goggles (gŏg′əlz) *n.* things you wear to protect your eyes during an experiment, **314**

gradual (grăj′o͞oəl) *adj.* slow, **106**

graduated cylinder (grăj′o͞o āt′əd sĭl′ən dər) *n.* a tool that helps measure volume or amount of a liquid, **311**

grains (grānz) *n.* tiny, hard parts that make up something larger, **94**

gram (grăm) *n.* a unit of mass, **160**

graphics (grăf′ĭks) *n.* images that support text in a book, **241**

graphs (grăfs) *n.* ways to organize information with bars, pictures, shapes, or lines, **216, 244**

grasslands (grăs′lăndz′) *n.* a biome covered by grasses and wildflowers, **69**

gravity (grăv′ĭ tē) *n.* a force that pulls objects towards one another, **194**

groundwater (ground′wôt ər *or* ground′wŏ tər) *n.* water that is collected in the soil, **125, 127**

grow (grō) *v.* become bigger, **30**

H

habitat (hăb′ĭ tăt) *n.* a place where an organism lives, **78, 84**

hazardous (hăz′ər dəs) *adj.* dangerous, **89**

headings (hĕd′ĭngz) *n.* words before text that tell you what the text is about, **241**

heart (härt) *n.* the organ that pumps blood around a body, **60**

heat energy (hēt ĕn′ər jē) *n.* the energy of particles in motion, **172**

hemisphere (hĕm′ĭ sfîr′) *n.* one half of Earth's surface, **149**

herbivores (hûr′bə vôrz *or* ûr′bə vôrz) *n.* animals that get all their energy by eating plants, **74**

homograph (hŏm′ə grăf *or* hō′mə grăf) *n.* a word with one spelling but more than one meaning, **282**

homophones (hŏm′fōnz *or* hō′ mə fōnz) *n.* words that have the same sound but different spellings and meanings, **280**

host (hōst) *n.* a living thing that a parasite lives off of for energy, **83**

humidity (hyo͞o mĭd′ĭ tē) *n.* the amount of water vapor in the air, **130**

humus (hyo͞o′məs) *n.* a layer of soil made up of the remains of dead plants, **116**

hurricane (hûr′ĭ kān *or* hŭr′ĭ kān) *n.* a large storm that forms over the ocean, **140**

hypothesis (hī pŏth′ĭ sĭs) *n.* a possible answer or explanation, **219**

I

idiom (ĭd′ē əm) *n.* a group of words that means something different when you put them together, **288**

igneous rock (ĭg′nē əs rŏk) *n.* a type of rock that forms when melted rock hardens, **96**

illustrations (ĭl ə strā′shənz) *n.* drawings used to explain things, **243**

image (ĭm′ĭj) *n.* a picture, **187, 258**

improve (ĭm prōōv′) *v.* make better, **304**

inclined plane (ĭn klīn′əd plān) *n.* a simple machine that is a ramp, **196**

index (ĭn′dĕks) *n.* a list of topics in a book, **239**

individuals (ĭn də vĭj′ōō əlz) *n.* the plural form of *individual,* meaning each living thing, **81**

infer (ĭn fûr′) *v.* make a conclusion by using information you observe or know, **214**

inference (ĭn′fər əns) *n.* a conclusion made by putting together what you know, **214, 256**

informal language (ĭn fôr′məl lăng′gwĭj) *n.* ways of speaking that are for settings that are not serious, **289**

information (ĭn fər mā′shən) *n.* facts or things you know, **216**

inherit (ĭn hĕr′ĭt) *v.* passing traits from parents to child, **46**

inner core (ĭn′ər kôr) *n.* the layer in the center of Earth made of solid metal, **92**

interact (ĭn tər ăkt′) *v.* have an effect or change one another, **73, 80**

intestines (ĭn tĕs′tĭnz) *n.* long, tube-like organs where most of digestion happens, **56**

invertebrates (ĭn vûr′tə brāts) *n.* animals that have no backbone, **21**

Glossary

Pronunciation Key

ă	bat	oi	toy
ā	ape	ou	shout
âr	**air**	ŏŏ	book
ä	father	ōō	moon
ĕ	let	s	sun
ē	easy	sh	pressure
ĭ	if	th	**the, thing**
ī	lie	ŭ	nut
îr	dear	ûr	circle
k	cause	ə	ago
ŏ	lot	ər	mother
ō	go	′	primary stress
ô	all	′	secondary stress

J

jargon (jär′gən) *n.* special words that are used by people with a certain hobby or in a certain profession, **286**

joint (joint) *n.* the place where bones come together, **54**

K

key term (kē tûrm) *n.* a vocabulary word, **242**

key words (kē wûrdz) *n.* words that you type into a search engine to find facts about a topic, **234**

kinetic energy (kĭ nĕt′ĭk ĕn′ər jē *or* kĭ nĕt′ĭk ĕn′ər jē) *n.* the energy of moving objects, **171**

kingdoms (kĭng′dəms) *n.* groups of different types of organisms, **18**

knowledge (nŏl′ĭj) *n.* information that you learn, **212**

L

landfills (lănd′fĭlz) *n.* the places where trash you throw away goes, **122**

landform (lănd′fôrm) *n.* a physical feature on Earth's surface, **102**

landslide (lănd′slīd) *n.* what happens when large amounts of rocks and soil slide or fall at once, **109**

lava (lä′və *or* lăv′ə) *n.* melted rock that rises through Earth's crust, **96**

layers (lā′ərz) *n.* things stacked on top of each other to create a whole, **92**

leaves (lēvz) *n.* the flat, green parts of a plant that stick out from the stem, **34**

lenses (lĕnz′əs) *n.* curved pieces of glass that refract light, **189**

lever (lĕv ər) *n.* a bar that turns around a point that doesn't move, **198**

light (līt) *n.* a form of energy that plants use to live, **32**; a form of energy that we use to see things, **186**

lightning (līt′nĭng) *n.* a giant spark in the sky during a thunderstorm, **139**

limbs (lĭmz) *n.* the legs, arms, or wings of an animal, **23**

limited (lĭm′ĭ tĭd) *adj.* not having an endless supply of something, **120**

liquid (lĭk′wĭd) *n.* the state of matter that takes the shape of whatever it is put in, **158**

liter (lē′tər) *n.* a unit used to measure volume, **161**

loam (lōm) *n.* soil made up of sand, clay, and humus, **116**

lungs (lŭngz) *n.* the parts in an animal's chest that help it breathe, **23, 58**

M

machine (mə shēn) *n.* a tool that makes work easier, **196**

magma (măg′mə) *n.* the hot, liquid substance that becomes igneous rock when it hardens, **96**

magnet (măg′nĭt) *n.* an object or material that attracts certain metals, such as iron, **182**

magnifying lens (măg′nə fī′ĭng lĕnz) *n.* a tool that makes objects look bigger, **311**

main idea (mān ī dē′ə) *n.* the most important point to understand, **252**

mammals (măm′əlz) *n.* warm-blooded animals that have a backbone and fur or hair, **23**

mantle (măn′tl) *n.* the layer of Earth between the crust and the core, **92**

mass (măs) *n.* the amount of matter in an object, **160**

matter (măt′ər) *n.* anything that has mass and takes up space, **156**

measure (mĕzh′ər) *v.* find out the amount of something, **211**

measuring cup (mĕzh′ə rĭng kŭp) *n.* a tool used for measuring liquids, **161**

melting (mĕl′tĭng) *n.* a physical change from solid to liquid, **166**

membrane (mĕm′brān) *n.* the part of a cell that gives it shape and controls what moves into and out of the cell, **50**

mesosphere (mĕz′ə sfîr *or* mĕs′ə sfîr) *n.* the coldest layer of Earth's atmosphere, **128**

metals (mĕt′lz) *n.* shiny and hard substances that conduct heat and electricity, **182**

metamorphic rock (mĕtē ə môr′fĭk rŏk) *n.* a type of rock that forms from heat and pressure, **97**

meteor (mē′tē ər *or* mē′tē ôr) *n.* a piece of rock from space that burns up as it goes into our atmosphere, **152**

meteorite (mē′tē ə rīt) *n.* a piece of rock from space that lands on Earth, **152**

meteorologist (mē tē ə rŏl′ə jĭst) *n.* a person who studies and predicts the weather, **137**

method (mĕth′əd) *n.* a plan of action, **218**

metric system (mĕt′rĭk sĭs′təm) *n.* a system of measurement used all over the world, **312**

mind (mīnd) *n.* the part of a person that thinks, feels, and understands, **258**

minerals (mĭn′ər əlz) *n.* solid, nonliving substances that form in the earth, **94**

misspell (mĭs spĕl′) *v.* spell wrong, **294**

monitor (mŏn′ĭ tər) *v.* check or keep track of, **262**

Moon (mo͞on) *n.* a large sphere that goes around Earth about once a month, **150**

motion (mō′shən) *n.* movement, **190**

mountain (moun′tən) *n.* a large mass of rock that sticks out high above Earth's surface, **103**

mouth (mouth) *n.* the part of the digestive system that allows you to take in and chew food, **56**

multiple meanings (mŭl′tə pəl mē′nĭngz) *n.* something that can be understood in different ways, **282**

muscles (mŭs′əl əs) *n.* the tissues attached to bones that make a body's parts move, **55**

muscular system (mŭs′kyə lər sĭs′təm) *n.* the group of parts that helps a body move, **55**

Glossary

Pronunciation Key

ă	bat	oi	toy
ā	ape	ou	shout
âr	**air**	o͝o	book
ä	father	o͞o	moon
ĕ	let	s	sun
ē	**ea**sy	sh	pressure
ĭ	if	th	**the, thing**
ī	lie	ŭ	nut
îr	**dear**	ûr	circle
k	cause	ə	ago
ŏ	lot	ər	moth**er**
ō	go	′	primary stress
ô	all	′	secondary stress

N

natural disaster (năch′ə rəl dĭ zăs′tər *or* năch′rəl dĭ zăs′tər) *n.* something that happens in nature that can harm people, **109**

natural resource (năch′ə rəl rē′sôrs′ *or* năch′ə rəl rĭsôrs′ *or* năch′rəl rē′sôrs′ *or* năch′rəl rĭsôrs′) *n.* any useful thing that is found in nature, **118**

negative charge (nĕg′ə tĭv chärj) *n.* one of the two types of electrical charges in matter, **178**

nerves (nûrvz) *n.* the things that carry messages between the brain and the other parts of a body, **63**

nervous system (nûr′vəs sĭs′təm) *n.* the group of parts that control how a body moves, **62**

niche (nĭch *or* nēsh) *n.* the role an organism plays in its habitat, **79**

nonrenewable resources (nŏn rĭnōō′ə bəl rē′sôrs′əs *or* nŏn rĭnōō′ə bəl rĭsôrs′əs) *n.* natural resources that cannot be replaced, **120**

nonvascular (nŏn văs′kyə lər) *adj.* having no tubes, **36**

nose (nōz) *n.* the part of the face that lets you smell and helps you breathe, **58**

note cards (nōt kärdz) *n.* small pieces of paper that you write notes on, **301**

notes (nōts) *n.* things you write down to help you remember information, **300**

nucleus (nōō′klē əs *or* nyōō′klē əs) *n.* the center of a cell that controls how the cell grows, **50**

nutrients (nōō′trē ənts *or* nyōō′trē ənts) *n.* something in food that organisms must have to live and grow, **32**

O

objects (ŏb′jĕkts′) *n.* things, **206**

observation (ŏb′zər vā′shən) *n.* something you notice, **214**

observe (əb zûrv′) *v.* look closely at, **206**

omnivores (ŏm′nə vôrz′) *n.* animals that get their energy from eating both plants and animals, **75**

orbit (ôr′bĭt) *v.* move around something in a path shaped like a circle, **144**

order (ôr′dər) *n.* an arrangement of things, **268**

organ (ôr′gən) *n.* a group of tissues in a body that work together to do a job, **52**

organelles (ôr′gə nĕlz′) *n.* the parts inside a cell that have special jobs, **50**

organisms (ôr′gə nĭz′əmz) *n.* living things, **18, 64**

organize (ôr′gə nīz′) *v.* put things in a way that is easy to find and understand, **302**

original (ə rĭj′ə nəl) *adj.* first; relating to the thing you started with, **292**

origins (ôr′ə jĭnz *or* ŏr′ə jĭnz) *n.* the places where things come from, **282**

outer core (out′ər kôr) *n.* the layer near the center of Earth made of liquid metal, **92**

outline (out′līn′) *n.* a short, written plan of what you are going to write or say later, **302**

oxygen (ŏk′sĭ jən) *n.* a gas in the air that animals must breathe to live, **28**

P

parasites (păr′ə sīts′) *n.* organisms that live off other organisms called hosts; parasites often harm their hosts, **83**

particles (pär′tĭ kəlz) *n.* tiny pieces that make up all matter, **164, 172**

parts (pärts) *n.* small things that make up large, whole things, **34**

patterns (păt′ərnz) *n.* models that show a relationship between things, **290**

pause (pôz) *v.* stop, **260**

periodicals (pĭr′ē ŏd′kəlz) *n.* things you read to find out information about current events; magazines and newspapers, **232**

petroleum (pə trō′lē əm) *n.* an oily liquid that can be burned to release energy, **121**

phases (fāz′əz) *n.* the different forms in a cycle, **151**

photographs (fō′tə grăfs′) *n.* pictures taken with a camera, **243**

photosynthesis (fō′tō sĭn′thĭ sĭs) *n.* a process where plants use the energy in sunlight to change carbon dioxide and water into food, **44**

phrasal verb (frāz′ ŭl vûrb) *n.* a verb plus one or more other words that makes a new verb, **292**

phrase (frāz) *n.* a group of words that works together, **292**

physical changes (fĭz′ĭ kəl chānj′ əs) *n.* what happens when the look of something changes, but no new kind of matter forms, **166**

pistil (pĭs′təl) *n.* the part of a flower that makes seeds, **43**

plain (plān) *n.* a wide area of flat or rolling land, **105**

plan (plăn) *v.* prepare a way of doing things, **302**

planet (plăn′ĭt) *n.* a large object that moves around the Sun, **144**

plates (plātəs) *n.* the parts that make up Earth's crust and solid upper mantle, **112**

poles (pōlz) *n.* ends, **183**

pollen (pŏl′ ən) *n.* the small grainy parts of a plant that help to make seeds, **42**

pollinate (pŏl′ə nāt′) *v.* cause a plant to reproduce, or make more plants, **42**

pollution (pə lōō′ shən) *n.* waste in the environment that causes the air, water, and land to be dirty, **89**

population (pŏp′ yə lā′ shən) *n.* all the organisms of the same kind that live in the same place, **65**

position (pə zĭsh′ ən) *n.* the place where something is, **190**

positive charge (pŏz′ĭ tĭv chärj) *n.* one of the two types of electrical charges in matter, **178**

potential energy (pə tĕn′ shəl ĕn′ ər jē) *n.* energy that is stored, **170**

precipitation (prĭ sĭp′ ĭ tā′ shən) *n.* a form of water that falls back to Earth, **127**

Glossary

Pronunciation Key

ă	bat	oi	toy
ā	ape	ou	shout
âr	**air**	o͝o	book
ä	father	o͞o	moon
ĕ	let	s	**sun**
ē	easy	sh	pressure
ĭ	if	th	**the, thing**
ī	lie	ŭ	nut
îr	**dear**	ûr	circle
k	cause	ə	ago
ŏ	lot	ər	moth**er**
ō	go	′	primary stress
ô	all	‚	secondary stress

precise (prĭ sīs′) *adj.* exact or correct, **304**

predator (prĕd′ə tər) *n.* a consumer that must eat other animals to get energy, **73**

predict (prĭ dĭkt′) *v.* use what you know or observe to say what will happen, **212, 250**

prediction (prĭ dĭk′ shən) *n.* a statement about what will happen in the future based on what you know, **136, 212**

prefix (prē′ fĭks′) *n.* a group of letters found at the beginning of a word or root, **276**

present (prĕz′ ənt) *v.* show, **244**

pressure (prĕsh′ ər) *n.* a force or push on something, **97, 131**

preview (prē′ vyo͞o′) *v.* look ahead, **233**

prey (prā) *n.* an animal a predator kills and eats, **73**

process (prŏs′ ēs′) *n.* the way that something happens, **44**; a number of steps, **205**

producers (prə do͞o′ sərz *or* pre dyo͞o′ srəz) *n.* living things that make their own food, **72**

products (prŏd′əkts) *n.* things that are made, **122**

professions (prə fĕsh′enz) *n.* the jobs people have, **286**

pronounce (prə nouns′) *v.* say out loud, **294**

pronunciation (prə nŭn′sē ā′shən) *n.* the way a word is said out loud, **279**

pronunciation key (prə nŭn′sē ā′shən kē) *n.* the part of a glossary that helps you say a word correctly, **238**

proofread (pro͞of′rēd) *v.* read something in writing to find and fix mistakes, **306**

properties (prŏp′ər tēz) *n.* special qualities or characteristics that describe things and events, **157, 206, 208**

pulley (po͞ol′ē) *n.* a simple machine made of a wheel and axle and a rope, **199**

punctuation (pŭngk′cho͞o a′shən) *n.* marks, like periods and commas, that help make writing easier to read, **306**

purpose (pûr′pəs) *n.* a goal or reason to do something, **231**

Q

questions (kwĕs′chəns) *n.* things you ask if you want answers, **204**

R

radar (rā′där) *n.* a tool that helps people predict the weather, **137**

radiation (ra′dē ā′shən) *n.* the movement of heat energy through space without using particles, **176**

rainwater (rān′wô′tər *or* rān′wôt′ər) *n.* water that comes down to Earth as rain, **125**

rays (rāz) *n.* thin lines of light that travel from the Sun or another energy source, **186**

react (rē ăkt′) *v.* respond to something, **62**

reasonable (rē′zə nə bəl) *adj.* making sense; thoughtful, **210**

recognize (rĕk′əg nīz′) *v.* understand; remember something from past experience, **268**

record (rĭ kôrd′) *v.* write down or store, **222**

recycle (rē sī′kəl) *v.* break down to use again, **76, 123**

reflect (rĭ flĕkt′) *v.* bounce back, **176, 187, 188**

refract (rĭ frăkt′) *v.* change direction, **189**

relate (rĭ lāt′) *v.* connect, **291**

relationship (rĭ la′shən shĭp) *n.* a connection between two or more things, **79, 82**

remains (rĭ mānz′) *n.* things that are left over, **100**

renewable resources (rĭ no͞o′ə bəl rē′sôrs′ əs *or* rĭ nyo͞o′ə bəl rē′sôrs′ əs) *n.* natural resources that are used and then replaced, **118**

repel (rĭ pĕl′) *v.* push apart by the physical force, **179**

report (rĭ pôrt′) *n.* a paper about what you learn, **224, 298**

reproduce (rē′prə do͞os′ *or* rē′prə dyo͞os′) *v.* make more of the same type of thing, **30, 42**

reptiles (rĕp′tīlz′ *or* rĕp′tĭlz) *n.* cold-blooded animals that have scales and a backbone, **26**

reread (rē′rēd) *v.* read something again, **263**

resources (rē′sôrs′ əz *or* rĭ sôrs′ əz) *n.* things that can be used to help living things, **81**

respiratory system (rĕs′pər ə tôr′ ē sĭs′təm *or* rĭ spīr′ə tôr′ ē sĭs′təm) *n.* the group of parts that help a body breathe, **58**

result (rĭ zŭlt′) *n.* something that happens in the end, **224**, **264**

retell (rē tĕl′) *v.* tell again, **254**

revise (rĭ vīz′) *v.* look at something to find ways to make it better, **304**

revolution (rĕv ə loo′shən) *n.* go around once, **149**

revolve (rĭ vŏlv′) *v.* move around something, **149**

rock (rŏk) *n.* a solid form that is made up of minerals and found on Earth's crust, **94**

role (rōl) *n.* a job, **34**

roots (roots) *n.* the parts of a plant that go into the soil, **34**

rotate (rō′tāt) *v.* spin, **146**

rule (rool) *n.* a direction that must be followed, **294**

ruler (roo′lər) *n.* a tool that helps measure lengths, **310**

rusting (rŭst′ĭng) *adj.* a chemical change that happens to metal, **169**

S

salt water (sôlt′ wô′tər *or* sôlt′ wŏt′ər) *n.* water that humans cannot drink; 97 percent of Earth's water, **124**

scales (skālz) *n.* the things that cover the bodies of fish and reptiles, **25**

scatter (skăt′ər) *v.* cause to fall in different places, **40**

scavengers (skăv′ən jərz) *n.* animals that eat dead animals that they did not kill, **75**

scientific method (sī′ ən tĭf′ĭk mĕth′əd) *n.* a plan for doing an experiment or finding out something, **218**

Glossary

Pronunciation Key

ă	bat	oi	toy
ā	ape	ou	shout
âr	**air**	oo	book
ä	father	oo	moon
ĕ	let	s	sun
ē	**ea**sy	sh	pressure
ĭ	if	th	**the, thing**
ī	lie	ŭ	nut
îr	**dear**	ûr	circle
k	cause	ə	ago
ŏ	lot	ər	**mother**
ō	go	′	primary stress
ô	**all**	′	secondary stress

scientists (sī′ən tĭsts) *n.* people who study the natural world, **205**

screw (skroo) *n.* an inclined plane wrapped around a tube, **197**

search (sûrch) *v.* look for, **234**

sediment (sĕd′ə mənt) *n.* loose pieces of rock and minerals that settle in layers, **98**

sedimentary rock (sĕd′ə mĕn′tə rē rŏk *or* sĕd′ə mĕn′trē rŏk) *n.* a type of rock that forms from layers of sediment that push down on other layers, **98**

seedlings (sēd′lĭngz) *n.* young plants that grow from seeds, **40**

senses (sĕns′əz) *n.* the five ways you take in information about the things around you, **206**

sequence (sē′kwəns) *n.* the order in which events happen, **268**

shadow (shăd′ō) *n.* the dark area that is created when rays of light are blocked by an object, **186**

shelter (shĕl′tər) *n.* a place to live, **28**

signal words (sĭg′nəl wûrdz) *n.* words in sentences that give clues about what you are going to read, **290**

similar (sĭm′ə lər) *adj.* the same as something else, **248**

skeletal system (skĕl′ĭ tl sĭs′təm) *n.* the group of bones that gives shape to a body, **54**

skeleton (skĕl′ĭ tn) *n.* a system of bones in a body, **54**

skill (skĭl) *n.* something you can do, **205**

slant (slănt) *v.* tilt, **146**

soil (soil) *n.* something in the ground made up of broken rocks and pieces of decayed matter, **116**

solar system (sō′lər sĭs′təm) *n.* the Sun and all the objects that orbit it, **144**

solid (sŏl′ĭd) *n.* the state of matter that has a defined shape; the particles in a solid are closer together than the particles in both liquids and gases, **158**

solution (sə lōō′shən) *n.* a mixture that looks like one substance, **167**

solve (sŏlv *or* sôlv) *v.* find an answer to a question or problem, **218**

sound (sound) *n.* something that can be heard, **184, 280**

sources (sôrs′əs) *n.* the places where things come from, **186**

space (spās) *n.* the endless area outside of Earth that holds solar systems, stars, and galaxies, **152**

Spanish (spăn′ĭsh) *n.* a language spoken in places such as Spain, Mexico, and many places in Central and South America, **278**

species (spē′shēz *or* spē′sēz) *n.* a group of living things that are alike in many ways, **19, 86**

speed (spēd) *n.* the measure of how quickly an object changes position, **191**

spellings (spĕl′ĭngz) *n.* the order of letters in a word, **280**

spinal cord (spī′nəl kôrd) *n.* a bunch of nerves that runs from the brain through the middle of the back, **63**

spores (spôrz) *n.* small cells that can become new plants, **39**

stages (stāgj′əz) *n.* steps in a cycle or process, **30**

stamen (stām′mən) *n.* the part of a flower that makes pollen, **43**

standard system (stăn′dərd sĭs′təm) *n.* the system of measurement used in the United States, **312**

star (stär) *n.* a thing in space that shines its own light, **153**

states (stāts) *n.* forms, **158**

static electricity (stăt′ĭk ĭ lĕk trĭs′ĭ tē *or* stăt′ĭk ē′ lĕk′ trĭs′ĭ tē) *n.* the form of energy that involves moving electric charges from place to place, **178**

stem (stĕm) *n.* the main part of a plant that holds up the leaves and flowers, **34**

stomach (stŭm′ək) *n.* an organ in the digestive system that uses its muscles to mix food with digestive juices, **56**

store (stôr) *v.* keep, **170**

storms (stôrmz) *n.* what can happen in the atmosphere when different air masses meet, **138**

strategy (străt′ə jē) *n.* method or plan of action, **256**

stratosphere (străt′ə sfîr) *n.* the layer of the atmosphere that is above the troposphere and below the mesosphere, **128**

stratus clouds (strā′təs kloudz′ or străt′əs kloudz′) *n.* layers of clouds that do not bring much rain, **133**

substance (sŭb′stəns) *n.* matter; something made of particles, **164**

suffix (sŭf′ĭks) *n.* a group of letters found at the end of a word, **276**

summarize (sŭm′ə rīz′) *v.* state only the most important ideas, **254**

summary (sŭm′ə rē) *n.* a few sentences about the key ideas in an article, **301**

superlative (soō pûr′lə tĭv) *n.* an adjective used to compare three or more things, **285**

support (sə pôrt′) *v.* give reasons to make something more believable, **252**

survive (sər vīv′) *v.* stay alive, **46**

symbiosis (sĭm′bē ō′sĭs or sĭm′bī ō′sĭs) *n.* a close relationship between two different species, **82**

system (sĭs′təm) *n.* a group of parts that work together, **53**

T

table of contents (tā′bəl ŭv kŏn′těnts′) *n.* the part of a book that names the units and chapters in order, **237**

technology (tĕk nŏl′ə jē) *n.* the useful tools that were made by scientists applying science ideas, **200**

temperature (tĕm′pər ə choōr′ or tĕm′prə choōr′) *n.* a measure of how fast the particles move in a substance, **173**

thermometer (thər mŏm′ĭ tər) *n.* a tool that measures temperature, **134**

thermosphere (thər′mō sfîr′) *n.* the layer of the atmosphere where temperature changes the most, **128**

threaten (thrĕt′n) *v.* put something in danger, **86**

thunder (thŭn′dər) *n.* the loud noise caused by lightning during a thunderstorm, **139**

thunderstorm (thŭn′dər stôrm′) *n.* a strong storm with lightning and thunder, **139**

time (tīm) *n.* the measure of how long it takes for an event to happen, **191**

tissues (tĭsh′oōs) *n.* groups of cells that work together to do the same kind of job, **52**

titles (tīt′lz) *n.* words at the top of a page or chart that tell you what the rest of the page or chart is about, **241**

topic (tŏp′ĭk) *n.* what something is about, **298**

tornado (tôr nā′dō) *n.* a fast-moving storm that forms over land, **142**

traits (trāts) *n.* characteristics or special things about an organism, **18**

transportation (trăns′pər tā′shən) *n.* a way to move from place to place, **201**

tropical rain forest (trŏp′ ĭ kəl rān′ fôr′ ĭst *or* trŏp′ ĭ kəl rān′ fŏr′ ĭst) *n.* a warm and wet biome where many different kinds of organisms live, **67**

troposphere (trō′ pə sfîr′ *or* trŏp′ əsfîr′) *n.* the layer of the atmosphere that is closest to Earth's surface, **128**

tubes (to͞obz *or* tyo͞obz) *n.* the round passages that move water through plants, **37**

tundra (tŭn′ drə) *n.* a cold and dry biome with a lot of snow and very few plants, **71**

U

units (yo͞o′ nĭts) *n.* small parts used to measure things, **211**; parts of a textbook that organize topics together, **230**

universe (yo͞o′ nə vûrs′) *n.* a huge collection of galaxies, **145**

V

valley (văl′ ē) *n.* a low, flat area of land between hills or mountains, **103**

variable (vâr′ ē ə bəl *or* văr′ ē ə bəl) *n.* something that can change, **221**

vascular (văs′ kyə lər) *adj.* having tubes that carry liquid, **37**

veins (vānz) *n.* the part of the circulatory system that carries blood from the body to the heart, **60**

vertebrates (vûr′ tə brāts) *n.* animals that have a backbone, **20**

vibrate (vī′ brāt) *v.* move back and forth, **184**

vibrations (vī brā′ shənz) *n.* what happens when things shake, or move back and forth, **114**

visualize (vĭzh′ o͞o ə līz′) *v.* make a picture in your mind of something, **258**

volcanoes (vŏl kă′ nō əs) *n.* a crack in Earth's crust that sometimes erupts and forms a hard landform, **110**

volume (vŏl′ yo͞om *or* vŏl′ yəm) *n.* the amount of space an object takes up, **161**

vortex (vôr′ tĕks′) *n.* air that spins or moves around in a path that is shaped like a circle and brings everything around it to its center, **142**

W

warm-blooded (wôrm′ blŭd′ ĭd) *adj.* having a body temperature that stays the same, **23**

waste chemicals (wāst kĕm′ ĭ kəlz) *n.* left over substances made of certain atoms; some waste chemicals can be harmful, **89**

water (wô′ tər *or* wôt′ ər) *n.* a liquid animals and plants must get to live, **28, 32, 45**

water cycle (wô′ tər sī′ kəl *or* wôt′ ər sī′ kəl) *n.* the constant movement of Earth's water from the surface to the air, back to the surface, **126**

water vapor (wô′ tər vā′ pər *or* wôt′ ər vā′ pər) *n.* water as a gas, **126**

wave (wāv) *n.* a ridge that moves across a body of water, **140**; a moving vibration that passes through the air, **184**

weather (wĕth′ ər) *n.* what is happening in the atmosphere, **134**

weathering (wĕth′ ər ĭng) *n.* the breaking down of landforms by the Sun, water, and wind, **106**

Web sites (wĕb′ sīts) *n.* pages on the Internet that have information about different topics, **234**

wedge (wĕj) *n.* an inclined plane turned on edge, **197**

weight (wāt) *n.* a measure of the force of gravity on an object, **195**

wheel and axle (hwēl ănd ăk′səl *or* wēl ănd ăk′səl) *n.* a simple machine that reduces friction and makes things easier to move, **196**

wind (wĭnd) *n.* moving air caused by differences in pressure, **131**

wind vane (wĭnd vān) *n.* a tool that measures wind direction, **135**

windpipe (wĭnd′pīp′) *n.* a tube to the lungs that air travels down to help you breathe, **58**

wings (wĭngz) *n.* the parts of a bird that help it fly or swim, **24**

work (wûrk) *v.* when force is applied to an object and the object moves, **196**

Glossary

Pronunciation Key

ă	bat	oi	toy
ā	ape	ou	shout
âr	**air**	o͝o	book
ä	father	o͞o	moon
ĕ	let	s	sun
ē	ea**s**y	sh	**pressure**
ĭ	if	th	**the, thing**
ī	lie	ŭ	nut
îr	**dear**	ûr	circle
k	cause	ə	ago
ŏ	lot	ər	mothe**r**
ō	go	′	primary stress
ô	all	′	secondary stress

Art Credits

Kenneth Batelman, p. **85**; Burgandy Beam, p. **177**; Linda Bittner, p. **28**; Annamarie Boley, pp. **35**, **37**; Denny Bond, p. **185**; Dan Bridy, pp. **112**, **113** *top, bottom,* **115**; Dusty Deyo, pp. **52** *left, middle, right,* **53**, **54**, **57**, **59**, **111**, **217** *top;* Jeff Grunewald, pp. **93**, **197** *top;* George Hamblin, pp. **132**, **147**, **149**, **151**, **176**; Michael Hortens, p. **159**; John Lambert, pp. **60**, **63**; Wendy Rasmussen, pp. **117**, **245**; Ronan Design, pp. **33**, **65**, **97**, **167**; Robert Roper, pp. **42**, **45**, **138**, **141**; Nadine Sokol, p. **51**.

Photo Credits

Cover: ©Brand X/Punch Stock; ©Getty Images; ©2007 iStock International Inc.; Oksana Perkins/Shutterstock, cover **front and back.**

©AGE, p. **143**; ©AGE Fotosearch, p. **19** *left;* ©Age Fotostock, pp. **46** *left,* **77** *bottom middle,* **202**, **214**, **262**; ©Alamy, pp. **43**, **66** *top right,* **70**, **95** *bottom,* **135** *left,* **108**; ©Glen Allison/Getty Images, pp. **66** *top left,* **67** *middle;* ©Altrendo Images/Getty Images, p. **193**; ©Colin Anderson/Getty Images, p. **208**; ©Atlantide Phototravel/Corbis, p. **21** *left;* ©Banana Stock/Punch Stock, p. **56**;

©Alistair Berg/Getty Images, p. **190**; ©Blend Images Photography/Veer, p. **11**; ©Brand X Pictures, p. **209** *middle right;* ©Brand X Pictures/Burke/Triolo Productions, p. **267**; ©Brand X/Jupiter Images, p. **194** *left;* ©Brand X/Punch Stock, pp. **27** *middle right,* **194** *right;* ©Mike Brinson/Getty Images, p. **124**; ©Simon Bruty/Getty Images, p. **191** *bottom;* ©Myrleen Ferguson Cate/Photo Edit, p. **310** *top;* ©Charles/Donnezan/Age Fotostock, p. **89**; ©David Chasey/Getty Images, p. **166** *bottom right;* ©Comstock/Punch Stock, p. **228**; ©Corbis, pp. **26** *left,* **40**, **263**; ©Daniel J. Cox/Corbis, pp. **22** *middle right,* **24** *top right,* **240** *middle right;* ©Andy Crawford/Dorling Kindersley, pp. **179**, **199**; ©Creatas/Punch Stock, pp. **66** *bottom left,* **71**, **87**, **122**; ©2007 Creative Force, Inc., p. **242**; ©Jim Cummins/Getty, pp. **58**, **314**; ©(DAL), pp. **188**, **233**, **260**; ©Tim Davis/Corbis, p. **24** *bottom;* ©Digital Vision, pp. **73**, **107**; ©Digital Vision/Getty Images, p. **274**; ©Digital Vision/Punch Stock, p. **86**; ©DK Limited/Corbis, p. **27** *left;* ©DLILLC/Corbis, pp. **5**, **22** *top,* **23**, **240** *top right,* **241** *top right;* ©Mike Dunning/Dorling Kindersley, pp. **146**, **147**, **148**, **149**; ©Ed-Imaging (DAL), p. **161** *top;* ©Gerry Ellis/Digital Vision, p. **75** *top;* ©Andrew Errington/Getty, p. **92**; ©Shannon Fagan/Getty Images, p. **276**;